GOOD

COMPANY

GOOD
COMPANY

ARTHUR M. BLANK

WILLIAM MORROW

An Imprint of HarperCollins*Publishers*

HarperCollins books may be purchased for educational, business, or sales promotional use. For information, please email the Special Markets Department at SPsales@harpercollins.com.

FIRST EDITION

Library of Congress Cataloging-in-Publication Data has been applied for.

ISBN 978-0-06-297492-1

20 21 22 23 24   LSC   10 9 8 7 6 5 4 3 2 1

To my family, and to the innumerable associates, past and present, who have brought these core values to life, inspiring and humbling me every step of the way.

To those who will read this book. May you lead with humility and laser-focus on building values-driven organizations that make the world a better place for all.

Contents

Foreword
by President Jimmy Carter

By trade, I am a carpenter and have worn a tool belt since the age of twelve. When I was a child growing up in an isolated peanut farming community, an occasional trip to the town hardware store with my father was a memorable adventure. In 1998, Rosalynn and I decided to renovate our kitchen, which had remained as it was since we first built our home in Plains, Georgia, some forty years previously. When the first Home Depot stores opened in Atlanta, it was an American craftsman's dream come true. I spent hours wandering the aisles, admiring bins of 16-penny nails and drill bits. When it came time to renovate our kitchen, we inquired about cabinetry. It was then that the store arranged for us to meet the owners, Arthur Blank and Bernie Marcus. Arthur's wife at that time, Stephanie, was a Home Depot designer and drew up the plans for the remodel. Arthur and I were brought together over kitchen accessories, but it soon became apparent that we had much more in common.

We both came from humble beginnings: I from rural Georgia; he from Sunnyside, Queens. We grew up with healers in our household: my mother, Lillian, a nurse; and his father, Max, a pharmacist. Our mothers were both dedicated community volunteers. We were raised in environments in which the foundation and highest spiritual essences of our Christian and Jewish faiths were valued over stigma and religious dogma. We were taught to exercise diplomacy to avoid conflict. What I have observed over two decades and now find most salient about Arthur is his sincerity, his integrity, and his relentless dedication to living his values. In a world often fixated on the quantification of things, Arthur effortlessly integrates that which cannot be counted into his life and work. Arthur knows what all servant leaders know: our communities are the bedrock of our country.

I long have been a Falcons fan, and while I've been thrilled to watch the team rise from mediocrity to become Super Bowl contenders, I've found it yet more exciting to watch an extremely successful American businessman maintain himself as a man of the people rather than as a sports oligarch on high.

The issues Arthur holds dear are central to me and to the Carter Center—health; peace and conflict resolution; the eradication of poverty; equality; and social justice. Arthur's philanthropic aims are grand within his own neighborhood, the city of Atlanta, the state of Georgia, and beyond. It is for this reason that he's sat on our board for the past twenty-five years and that we've asked him to help us with succession planning and to ensure the continuation of our work beyond our lifetimes.

The growing chasm between rich and poor is one of our nation's biggest challenges. There is no way to separate this from the basic rights of food, health, security, and human dignity. The work of the Arthur M. Blank Family Foundation on Atlanta's historic Westside is perhaps the greatest example in the American South—maybe even in all of America—of a meaningful effort to bridge a daunting socioeconomic chasm.

Witnessing the positive economic and social change he's set in motion in his own backyard—which happens to be the birthplace of our nation's civil rights movement—has given me hope that as a country we'll return to an understanding of what service and leadership truly mean.

I have faith in humanity because I know people like my friend Arthur Blank, people who see things that require attention, hard work, collaboration, and mindfulness and who have the passion to keep participating in ways that are truly helpful and supportive; people who represent the highest ideals of being a servant leader.

People have asked of Arthur and me: When does the work end for you? The answer is: it doesn't. The work is just beginning. We all are presented with the choice to mend the world, to bring it one step closer toward a harmonious state of being. I invite you to take note of the story of this fine American who chose to do just that.

President Jimmy Carter

Plains, Georgia

March 2020

Acknowledgments

You're only as good as your people—this has proven to be true in every one of my business and nonprofit ventures, and this book has been no exception. I could not have produced it without the commitment and creativity of the many talented associates and partners who have guided and supported me along the way. I hesitated to embark on this journey at first, knowing what an enormous commitment it takes to write and produce a book. My exceptional team made it not only easy but even enjoyable.

Brett Jewkes was the earliest champion of this project, believing its message would be important now and in generations to come. I am deeply grateful he persisted, despite my reluctance, and has remained a passionate steward of the project from start to finish.

Lara Fawaz was indispensable. She did an outstanding job as project manager, juggling multiple schedules with grace and diplomacy, keeping everything on track, and ensuring that all the right people were included in the process.

Sarah Grigg's tremendous contribution to this work began when it was only an idea. As someone whose writing about our ranches touched me deeply, she was the person I turned to for invaluable help in creating the book proposal for what would become *Good Company*, and my gratitude for her part in this journey is full.

The best decision I made on this project was selecting Ellen Daly to be my writing partner. Her intuitive understanding of the core values and almost-spiritual connection to my vision for this book from the start have made all the difference. Her talent and skill will always be remembered, but it is the creation of a lifelong friendship with her that I will cherish most.

Dozens of my associates, colleagues, friends, and family generously gave of their time to share stories, review drafts, and check facts. The book is much richer as a result of their contribution, and I am grateful to all of them for being a part of the process.

From the moment this book was conceived, it has been guided by the shrewd judgment of my agents at Aevitas Creative, David Granger and Todd Shuster. I am deeply appreciative of their commitment to the book and thankful for their wise counsel and integrity from the start. I'm also grateful they connected us with Mauro DiPreta and the team at William Morrow. We could not have asked for better publishing partners. Mauro's thoughtful editing and personal enthusiasm for the book's message have made for a seamless collaboration at every step of the way. I am also indebted to Mike Egan and Melissa Altman for always bringing their expertise to our family of businesses and the agreements that made this work possible; to retired Home Depot SVP of Marketing Dick Hammill for his meticulous proofreading; to Arnica Spring Rae for her masterful photography (and patience with me during the process); and to the AMBSE Creative Design team for its work on the book's cover.

Every day, I am thankful for the dedicated staff in the Arthur M. Blank Family Office, who keep my complicated life running smoothly. In particular, I want to thank Janet Lathrop, Laura Moore, and Victoria Pence for coordinating so many of the logistics of getting this work done.

Finally, I am honored that President Carter agreed to grace this book with a Foreword. As a humanitarian, he has no peer. As a caring friend, he is unmatched.

A question I have asked myself about every one of my businesses is this: Are we, as a company, worthy of our people's lives? Are we honoring the time, the commitment, and the life energy that they bring to their jobs every day? I ask myself the same question about this book. My sincerest hope is that it will prove to be worthy of all the hard work and creativity that so many people have contributed along the way, giving them, and the people who read these pages, the sense that they are part of something truly meaningful that can make a difference in this world.

Introduction

One of the unexpected benefits of being a successful business leader in the later stages of life is that I get to go back to school. Not as a student (although I do consider every visit a learning opportunity) but as a speaker. I'm regularly invited to business school campuses to address aspiring entrepreneurs and future executives about what I've learned in my many decades building values-based companies. I consider this a great privilege. The young people I meet during these visits strike me as deeply thoughtful, motivated, and creative, and I always leave feeling encouraged that they are about to step into our country's offices and boardrooms.

They also strike me as worried and frustrated. They're keenly aware of the challenges facing our environment; the gaps in wealth and opportunity; the gender-wage discrepancy; the persistent discrimination faced by minorities both in the workplace and outside; and the numerous examples of corporate misconduct. I have college-aged children of my own, and I hear the same concerns around the dinner table. They're searching for better solutions, new approaches, fresh answers. If there's one question I hear above all others from the business school students I meet, it's this: Does my choice to pursue a career in business conflict with my need for meaning and purpose and my desire to make a positive difference in the world?

I'll be honest—I don't think I was asking such deep or thoughtful questions on the day I walked across the stage in my cap and gown at Babson College in 1963. My demeanor was more carefree, my focus more singular. I had few advantages beyond my own smarts and willingness to work hard, but I was optimistic and full of confidence in my ability to change my own circumstance. Much of this came from my family. My grandparents all came to the United States from Europe with little more than the clothes on their backs, and they made their way in this country however they could. My grandfather used to carry furniture up the stairs for people in his neighborhood in order to earn extra money to supplement the income he made as a fishmonger at the Essex Street Fish Market on New York's Lower East Side. My family was living in a one-bedroom apartment in Queens, New York, when my father launched his own pharmaceutical mail-order company at the age of forty. And when he passed away only four years later, my mother, who had no prior business experience, stepped up and took over the company, building it into a thriving million-dollar business while raising my brother and me alone. Inspired by these examples of resilience and resourcefulness, I helped support myself during my college years by launching a landscaping business and a laundry business.

After graduating, I took an accounting job for five years at Arthur Young & Company, before joining the family business. When my mother sold that business to the national conglomerate Daylin Corporation, I stayed with the company and worked my way up, eventually becoming president of their drugstore division while still in my twenties. When that division was sold off, a friend named Bernie Marcus, who worked at another Daylin subsidiary, Handy Dan Home Improvement Centers, hired me as chief financial officer. That was the beginning of one of the most important professional and personal relationships of my life. Bernie, fourteen years my senior, became like both a father and a brother to me. We had an instant rapport.

Bernie has a strong personality, to put it mildly, and he is a great businessman. Our personalities are complementary— he's a natural entertainer and visionary; I'm more reserved, cautious, and analytical. To use a baseball analogy, he's the pitcher, the center of attention, while I'm the catcher, in the middle of the action and helping set the pace of the game. We've always brought out the best in each other and have great respect for each other's strengths. Unfortunately, the same could not be said of our corporate overlords at Daylin, who wanted to take all the credit for Handy Dan's outstanding performance. On April 14, 1978, the growing friction came to a head. Bernie, myself, and another close colleague, Ron Brill, were summoned to a planning meeting at the corporate offices. Upon arrival, we were shuttled into separate rooms, each containing several attorneys, and fired on the spot.

Getting fired by Daylin was a shock, but it turned out to be the best thing that could have happened to us. In the weeks that followed, at a Los Angeles coffee shop halfway between our homes, Bernie and I first sketched out a business plan for a new store we would come to call The Home Depot.

That business, which we cofounded with retailer Pat Farrah and financier Ken Langone, went on to become the leading home improvement retailer in the world, with an unparalleled track record of growth. During my twenty-three years with the company (1978–2001), we grew from an idea and a dream to almost 1,500 stores, more than 250,000 associates, and a valuation of $50 billion. But my proudest moment, among all

the successes we celebrated and accolades we received, was
when a Harris Interactive survey in 2001 voted us America's most socially responsible company. The fact that we were
given this honor was deeply meaningful to me, but even more
so was the fact that we accomplished this while at the same
time achieving a compound annual growth rate of 46 percent,
49 percent growth in earnings, and 45 percent growth in stock
price. When the young people I meet today ask me whether
their business ambitions conflict with their need for meaning,
purpose, and impact, I cite those numbers, because to me the
story of The Home Depot is the most convincing proof I have
that purpose and profit can—and should—beautifully coexist.

However, this book is not just that story.* It's also the story
of what happened next. As the old saying goes, once is chance,
twice is a coincidence, three times is a pattern. Was The Home
Depot a one-off—a fortuitous combination of timing, concept,
market, and people that added up to retail magic? Or could
the essence of what made that company great be replicated—
in other settings, other industries, and with a different cast of
characters? That was the question I faced when I left the company in 2001, still relatively young, healthy, ambitious, and inspired to create value for myself and my community. Would
I be able to take the values on which we'd built The Home
Depot and use them to transform other companies and start
new ones? Would they translate out of retail into other sectors?
Would they prove to be as enduring as I believed them to be?

---

* For the Home Depot story, see Arthur Blank and Bernie Marcus,
*Built from Scratch: How a Couple of Regular Guys Grew The Home Depot
from Nothing to $30 Billion.*

This book tells the story of how I set out to do just that—to use the values that built The Home Depot to shape and lead a variety of organizations, including a long-established but struggling National Football League (NFL) team, a brand-new stadium, a startup Major League Soccer team, a near-bankrupt retail chain, a guest ranch, a nonprofit retreat center, and a family foundation. I'll share the challenges, successes, and surprises that have accompanied every step of the journey, as well as the lessons I've learned along the way about leadership, innovation, growth, service, crisis management, giving back, and more. In the process, I hope to dispel at least a little of the pervasive cynicism about the nature of business and inspire the leaders of today and tomorrow to embrace a values-based approach.

That being said, I know that the path that lies ahead of today's young entrepreneurs is different than the one I walked. In the decades since I began my journey in business, the world has changed unimaginably, and confidence in institutions has steadily fallen. According to Gallup, more than half of Americans believe that corruption is widespread in business,[1] and a recent Pew Research Center report ranked big business near the top of the list of institutions people don't trust to act in the best interests of the public, surpassed only by elected officials.[2] In our hyperconnected world, we all face far greater public scrutiny at a time when the expectations of business and its leaders have risen significantly. Business leaders today have more factors to take into consideration than they did a half century ago. They need to be more sensitive, more informed, more nimble, more creative, and more courageous. Yet while the world changes around us, the values that create a good company have proven, in my experience, to be the same today as they were when I started out. Caring for customers, treating associates with respect, being inclusive, fostering innovation, giving back to the community, leading by example—these are the attitudes that differentiate the businesses that thrive over the long term, and even more so in today's challenging climate. They're equally important in other sectors too—in education, politics, nonprofits, and more.

My greatest hope for this book is that it will be read by the leaders not only of today but of the future—young people like those I meet on college campuses and in our businesses— and that it will fuel their optimism and commitment. I hope that they will come away with a new confidence that their desire to succeed in business does not have to be at odds with their desire to live lives of meaning and purpose. In fact, quite the opposite. By marrying those two drives, they can have a far greater impact in the world than they might if they were to pursue either one at the expense of the other. If we are to meet the tremendous challenges that face us, we need to harness the ambition, the creative minds, the entrepreneurial spirit, and the capacity for risk-taking that have always defined capitalism at its best. The leaders of today and tomorrow have an extraordinary opportunity: to prove that through upholding values we can create value—for the company, for the customer, and for the community.

Chapter 1

||||||||||||||||||||

Family Business

*Through our scientific and technological genius we've
made of this world a neighborhood. And now through
our moral and ethical commitment we must make of it a
brotherhood.*

—Dr. Martin Luther King Jr.

Oes Pharmacy was a family business. Locals stopped by the
store on the corner of Forty-Seventh and Queens Boulevard in
Sunnyside, New York, to get their prescriptions filled or to pick
up a jar of face cream. My uncle Sam owned the place, having bought it from its founder, Willy Oes, and he and my dad
worked behind the counter, mixing tinctures, grinding powders, and filling capsules. But their job involved much more
than dispensing drugs. Those were the days when druggists
were often de facto community medical counselors. Dad and
Uncle Sam knew the name and common ailments of every
customer who walked through their door—from Mr. Arnold's
goiter to old Miss Zuckerman's arthritis—and were there to
provide advice, as well as the liniment or pills that would re-
lieve the discomfort. One day, as Dad told it, a distraught young
woman walked in and burst into tears, confessing that she was

pregnant. When he inquired as to why she had come to this conclusion, she whispered that she'd kissed a boy. Dad sat her down and gently set her straight on a few facts of life.

I loved accompanying my mother as she delivered egg sandwiches to Dad for his lunch. As a toddler, I wandered across the linoleum floors, mesmerized by bright jars of Brylcreem and boxes of candy, fat bags of Epsom salts and bottles of boric acid. When I was old enough, I delivered Dad's lunch myself and sat and watched for hours while he mixed prescriptions, decanted cough medicine into smaller bottles, and wrote the details of each transaction by hand in one of his large ledgers. I was born too late to remember the days when the pharmacy had a soda fountain, but my older brother, Michael, assures me it once did. It also had a pay phone and a resident bookie who ran his business from the booth. The window displays enticed customers with colorful rows of lipsticks and elegant glass bottles. The ads that plastered the walls announced treatments for everything from everyday exhaustion to intractable hiccups to belligerent senior citizens. But as I look back now, I realize that it wasn't any of those products or promises that kept the pharmacy filled with people—talking, laughing, socializing, in no hurry to resume the business of the day. They may have come for the items on their shopping lists—for pills, powders, or potions—but they stayed for the company.

A good company becomes a community. The word *company* means fellowship or companionship, and the best businesses treat their customers like honored guests (another fitting meaning of the term *company*). Many people look back nostalgically to businesses like my uncle Sam's and bemoan the loss of those mom-and-pop shops and the sense of community they fostered. They blame the growth of market capitalism, the influx of big-box stores, and the shift to online retail for driving out small businesses and leaving neighborhoods without those hubs of connection, familiarity, and support. But I don't think it has to be that way. My own path took me from helping out in the family pharmacy to cofounding the largest home improvement retailer on the planet, The Home Depot. By the time I left, in 2001, we employed more than 250,000 people (it's now 400,000). And you know what? Every one of those stores felt as much like a community as that little pharmacy on the corner in Queens. It's not size that makes the difference; it's attitude. If customers feel as though they're interacting with human beings who care, rather than with an institution, it doesn't matter how big the company as a whole might be. Large does not have to mean impersonal. If a business truly sees itself as a community—both for its customers and for the people who work there—it will infuse its everyday activities with a spirit of hospitality.

It's understandable that people might balk at hearing business described in such noble terms. We live in an era when confidence in institutions has plummeted, with close to half the population saying they distrust businesses, according to the annual Edelman Trust Barometer.[1] From the Enron collapse at the turn of the millennium, to the 2008 financial crisis, to today's tech giant data scandals, corporate misconduct looms larger than ever in the public awareness. Many have come to the conclusion that the profit motive inherently corrupts and that capitalism itself is a flawed system based on greed and competition. Unfortunately, such sentiments find plenty of backup in the daily news cycle. If you want to find corporate bad actors, you don't have to look far. The stories we hear less frequently are those in which businesses strive to succeed while also making a positive difference in the world.

Those stories do exist, however, and we need to hear more of them. Businesses can and *should* do great things. They can be part of the solution, not the problem. In fact, because corporations wield so much power and influence in our society, they have an unmatched opportunity to do good, for the people who work in them and for the communities in which they do business. I'm not just talking about adding a few benefits and engaging in a little philanthropy on the side; I'm suggesting that doing good becomes an integral part of business activities. When we leverage our business interests for the greater good of our people's lives and our community's well-being while at the same time increasing profit, business and philanthropy become inseparable.

I think of it as lifting both sides of the barbell. You can't lift, squat, and overhead press a great weight from just one side, either from under the plates of capitalism or from under the plates of social responsibility. You have to get your entire body centered under that bar to propel it skyward, balancing the reality of the need for profitability with the challenges facing communities, our nation, and the world.

This is the essence of what I call "good capitalism," which has also been called "conscious capitalism," "conscious business," or "the triple bottom line" (people, planet, profits). It's an approach to business that elevates the interests of all stakeholders—from shareholders to vendors to customers to associates to community members to the local environment. Whatever name we give it, there's no question in my mind that this approach to business represents a much-needed paradigm shift from conventional thinking. And it's catching on. In the summer of 2019, Business Roundtable released a new Statement on the Purpose of a Corporation, which was signed by 181 CEOs, including the leaders of dozens of major national and international companies. The essence of their statement was that businesses are no longer primarily responsible to shareholders; they are responsible to all stakeholders, including customers, associates, communities, suppliers, and the environment as well. As my good friend Jamie Dimon, chairman of Business Roundtable and chairman and CEO of JPMorgan Chase & Co., puts it, "Major employers are investing in their workers and communities because they know it is the only way to be successful over the long term. These modernized principles reflect the business community's unwavering commitment to continue to push for an economy that serves all Americans."[2]

Change is not always welcomed, however. When I've made decisions that depart from business-as-usual, I've upset my competitors, been told by my friends that I'm crazy, and had many moments when I wondered if I'd been naïve or foolish. I've been viewed with suspicion and worse by people in the very communities I hoped to uplift. I've found myself at the center of media storms and highly contentious national debates. I've watched as decades of hard work were undone by those who didn't share my values, and I've been forced to reflect on how fragile even the best company can be. But I've learned invaluable lessons from every one of these challenging moments, and again and again I've had successes and breakthroughs that inspire and motivate me to continue.

More and more companies are discovering the power of doing well by doing good, and I hope and expect to see many more follow suit in the decades to come—because it's good citizenship *and* good business. It's time we get beyond the idea that profit and purpose are at odds and embrace the more empowering truth that when a good company does well, it benefits everyone.

This truth was at the heart of The Home Depot's approach

and fueled its extraordinary accomplishments, from the opening of the first handful of stores in 1979 through the twenty-
plus-year run of 40 percent annual growth led by cofounders
Bernie Marcus and myself, to its continued success today.
It's that very same philosophy—the marriage of purpose and
profit—that informs my "family of businesses" today, which
includes two professional sports teams (the NFL's Atlanta Falcons and MLS's Atlanta United), a seventy-one-thousand-seat
sports and entertainment venue (Mercedes-Benz Stadium),
the largest golf specialty retail chain in the world (PGA TOUR
Superstore), the Arthur M. Blank Family Foundation, and
three Montana ranches (Mountain Sky Guest Ranch, West
Creek Ranch, and Paradise Valley Ranch). Each of these very
different enterprises is guided by the same principles and core
values. And each of them, like my uncle's pharmacy, is a community.

Circles of Impact

Community, for a good company, does not just mean the people within its own walls or on its block. In fact, its influence

THE BLANK FAMILY *of* BUSINESSES	Atlanta Falcons
	PGA TOUR Superstore
	Atlanta United
	Mercedes-Benz Stadium
	Mountain Sky Guest Ranch
	West Creek Ranch
	Paradise Valley Ranch
	The Arthur M. Blank Family Foundation
	AMB Sports & Entertainment
	AMB Family Office

ripples out like a series of concentric circles. The innermost circle includes the company's associates (a term we use for everyone who works in our businesses), as well as the people they are serving—customers, fans, or guests. The middle circle is the local community in which the company is situated— the street, neighborhood, or city that it calls home. And the largest circle encompasses the entire industry within which the business is situated, and perhaps even broader sectors of society. Of course, these are not always separate, distinct constituencies. In reality, they overlap and build on one another, amplifying impact in the process. The beauty of these widening circles of impact is that there's a constant interaction between them. For example, a company that hires from its local community turns neighbors into associates. Associates who get involved in initiatives in the local community and beyond find themselves making an impact that further inspires and engages them with their company. And companies that do well by doing right by their customers will sooner or later catch the attention of their competitors and begin to influence their industries. In the chapters ahead, you'll find stories and examples that show how truly integrated all of these efforts to do good can be. But before we get there, let's take a closer look at the opportunity for impact in each of these circles.

Associates and Customers: Creating Connection

What makes a good company, regardless of the industry in which it operates, is its ability to facilitate human connection. Now that I'm in my eighth decade of life, I am firmly con-

vinced that the simple act of connecting to other human beings is the key to personal happiness and health as well as to a
thriving business. But even though I couldn't have named it at
the time, it's the exact thing I felt as a young boy, sitting at the
counter in Oes Pharmacy, watching my father minister to the
neighborhood. It's what drew me to play and watch sports as
a child, and to invest in the business of sports as an adult. It's
what I felt when I walked the floors of any Home Depot store,
greeted by smiling associates and loyal customers. It's what
matters most to me in any of my business or philanthropic endeavors: the deepening and widening of our circles of human
connection.

A good company has the opportunity to do something that
is often overlooked in business plans or MBA programs: it
can make people happier. Not just through providing goods
or services that improve the quality of lives (although that's
important too) but in the very act of doing business. There's
a magic that can happen every single day in the interactions
within its closest circle of community: the associates and the
customers. A company can touch customers' hearts, minds,
and spirits with great service and, in the process, give associates the feeling that there's a purpose to what they're doing.
They're not just engaging in a transaction; they're building a
relationship, and relationships are the most important things
in life, as both ancient wisdom and modern science tell us.
For this reason, I've never really thought of myself as being
in the business of home improvement, professional sports,
stadium management, guest ranching, or sports retail. I'm
in the business of human happiness. I consider it part of my
purpose in life to increase the happiness of others, and all

of my many business ventures are outlets for this purpose. Our associates know it too, and that's why they love to work with us. And our customers, our guests, and our fans let us know that we're doing a good job in the best way possible: they come back.

Initially, they may have come to us for something specific— the spectacular architecture and innovative technology of our stadium, the selection of products at our stores, the stunning scenery at our ranches, the entertaining talents of our sports teams. They may have come to see a great game and enjoy a beer and a hot dog; to buy a new set of golf clubs; to learn to ride a horse. But after a few visits, those things inevitably lose a little of their shine. What keeps people coming back is the experience they have and the connections they make as they interact with our associates. They stay for the company.

Local Community: Leading Change

When I left The Home Depot, I never intended to leave Atlanta. In fact, one of my overriding desires was to give back to the city that had launched our company and made it such a success. Whatever new endeavors lay ahead of me, they would be embedded in that community and dedicated to improving it in the best way I knew: by doing good business there.

Every company, large or small, has an opportunity and a responsibility to do good in its own neighborhood. That might mean a small town, a city block, or a rural community, or it might mean a whole city. In the most basic sense, simply setting up shop in a community is a chance to bring jobs, services, and other economic opportunities to the people who live there. A good company thinks about its location not just as something to exploit for profit or cost savings but as a strategic opportunity to serve. When I decided to build our new stadium downtown, just a stone's throw from Atlanta's historic Westside, I did so because I saw a chance to uplift that community as well as to infuse our teams and our sports with the energy of transformation that makes our city great. It wasn't an easy choice, nor was it always a popular one, but it has benefited both our business and that community in countless ways and will for decades to come.

The same can be true at any scale when companies begin to look outside their own walls and fences and find ways to get involved in the neighborhood. It might mean sponsoring and getting involved in community projects; creating job-training programs and recruiting local residents; providing space for community events; spearheading local change efforts; or encouraging other businesses to move to the neighborhood.

Industry and Society: Modeling Potential

One of my core values is leading by example, and this applies both to people and to companies. A good company can set an example—for others in its industry, and perhaps even beyond, for society as a whole. When a company takes a risk to do the right thing and is rewarded by improvements in revenue and reputation, it can give others the courage to do the same. Many businesses are risk-averse, and they don't necessarily want to go first, but if they have an example to model themselves after, they're more likely to change. Sometimes this happens simply through comparison; other times the pressure to change comes from customers who notice the difference in one business and begin to demand the same from its competitors. When we dramatically reduced our pricing for food and drinks at Mercedes-Benz Stadium, some of our partners and most of our competitors weren't happy. Now, they're lining up to learn about our fan-friendly model, and many are implementing it themselves.

Just as a company can inspire change in its competitors, it can also put pressure on entire industries—improving environmental impact, work conditions, or quality standards down the supply chain. When The Home Depot decided to sell only sustainable lumber in 1999, it was the beginning of a journey for the whole industry to understand and embrace better forestry.

On a societal level, companies have a prominent platform and can have an impact far beyond their own industry. In several instances, I've found myself and my businesses at the heart of polarizing national debates on issues like race, human rights, animal welfare, and gentrification. It's my job, and the responsibility of my companies, to not shy away from such moments, but to strive for grace and diplomacy in addressing these issues. Businesses have a unique opportunity to rise above the political fray and seek values-driven solutions that constructively move things forward.

My Guiding Light

At this stage of my life, my kids are probably right when they gently encourage me to slow down a little, but retirement is the last thing on my mind. My work and my family are what keep me feeling alive. Every day, I'm inspired and motivated by the people I work with; the customers, fans, and guests we serve; and the ripples of impact our companies and foundation make in the world. But when I think about what deeply drives me in all my endeavors, both commercial and philanthropic, my mind goes back to my family and to our family business. My dad, Max Blank, serving our neighbors at the pharmacy, and later running his own mail-order pharmaceutical company. My mother, Molly Blank, who took over Dad's business after he passed away when I was fifteen and built it into a successful company, despite having no business background. Mom was an artist, a universalist, and a social justice warrior who pushed her children to learn about other religions and cultures while fiercely adhering to her Jewish roots. Part of the reason my children and I are so interested in social challenges and the happiness of our society comes, without a doubt, from my mother. She truly lived by *tikkun olam,* the ancient Jewish teaching that each of us is capable of acts of kindness to improve and repair the world. And she was a woman of undying principle.

In situations when a small injustice occurred and others would have just let it go or turned a blind eye, Molly would always keep fighting. Even if the sum of money or the number of people involved seemed inconsequential, she wouldn't back down. Sometimes I'd say to her, "Mom, it's not worth it!" But she'd shake her head and declare, "It's the principle of the thing!" She was always generous with those in need, even when we had very little to give. She never hesitated to speak up for what she believed to be right, whether it was a trifling dispute or a life-threatening situation.

As an example of the latter, one Friday evening when I was about ten years old, I heard a crash in the foyer of our apartment, which doubled as my parents' bedroom. When I walked out to see what was happening, the front door was wide open and my father was kneeling on the floor. Two men were aiming a gun at his head. They had followed him from the pharmacy, mistakenly believing that he took the cash home for the weekend. One of the robbers herded Michael, my mother, and me into the living room and made us sit on the floor, while the other marched my father around the small apartment, demanding to know where the money was kept. It didn't take long, since there were only four rooms— the foyer, the kitchen, the bathroom, and the bedroom where Michael and I slept.

I was scared, and I could tell that Michael was too, but if my mother was afraid, she didn't show it. In fact, in her most principled tone, she gave that robber a lecture on how wrong this was and how he needed to find something else to do for a living before he ended up hurting himself and other people. "What would your mother think if she could see you like this?" She went on and on, trying to reform this guy who was sitting there with a gun across his lap. Was it the best idea, given the circumstances? Probably not. But it was the principle of the thing that mattered! She saw an opportunity to repair a particular piece of the world, and she was going to do her best to do so. Finally, he said to her, quite calmly, "Look, I get it, lady. I understand. Now would you please shut up?"

After thoroughly searching the apartment but finding no cash, his partner came back, frustrated. The guy who'd been guarding us ordered me to get in the bathtub, where he tied me up. I decided this was as good a time as any to use all the worst words I knew, so I started cursing him out. I'll never forget the look on his face when he said, "You're not supposed to be talking that way. I'm going to go tell your mother, and she'll wash your mouth out with soap!" Clearly, her principles had made an impression.

I owe much of my own principled approach to life and business to the early impression my mother made upon me, both in her personal convictions and in her Jewish faith. I try to live by the guiding light of *tikkun olam* as I go about my own work. And I believe that companies—good companies—can play an outsized role in that sacred effort to repair the world and lift up humanity. In doing what's right by your customers, your associates, your community, and society as a whole, your business can become an agent of change. If you establish and tirelessly maintain a culture of doing good, you will without a doubt do well, for yourself and for the larger community. Commercial success does not have to come at the cost of community, relationships, and happiness—it can and should arise *because* of those things.

Today, I have tremendous confidence in this new formula for success, because I've seen it proven again and again, in diverse business environments from retail to hospitality to sports and entertainment. But on the day I left The Home Depot in 2001, I had nothing to go on but my experience building and leading that one company. We'd been successful beyond our wildest dreams and created a business and a community that I was proud of. But would the values we'd worked so hard to nurture survive my departure? And would they prove to be the universal principles I believed them to be? Would I be able to re-create that values-driven, people-focused culture somewhere else?

Chapter 2

‖‖‖‖‖‖‖‖‖‖‖‖‖

Everything Changes but the Values

We must adjust to changing times and still hold to unchanging principles.

—PRESIDENT JIMMY CARTER

In a daze, I stumbled out of the aircraft hangar conference room onto the tarmac. February is one of the most pleasant times of year in Florida, but I hardly noticed the warm breeze or the soft evening light. It was 2001, and I'd just attended a meeting of the Home Depot board of directors at which I had been told, in no uncertain terms, that it was time for me to leave the company I'd cofounded, built, and led for twenty-three years. My part in the Home Depot story was abruptly over.

This wasn't the way it was supposed to end. The whole evening felt like a surreal interlude—as if I could just step back onto the waiting plane and return to the real world and none of this would have happened. When I arrived home and told my wife, Stephanie, her disbelief mirrored my own. As she realized I wasn't kidding, she was outraged over the treatment I'd been shown.

I just felt sad—for myself, but even more so for the company, our associates, and our leadership team. What hurt and disappointed me was not the idea of moving on from the company—I'd already decided that I was ready for a change and had informed the board several months earlier of my intentions. It was the unexpected and unpleasant way it happened. And even worse, it was the sinking feeling I got when I considered the hands in which I was leaving my baby.

The Home Depot really was like a child to me. I'd hoped for, and expected, a very different kind of transition. I'd taken over from Bernie as CEO in 1997, when he moved into an executive chairman role. When I decided it was time for me too to move on, I'd chaired the search committee myself, carefully considering possible successors. I wished there was someone internally we could promote, but in this respect the company was a victim of its own success: our best people had become so wealthy that they'd decided to retire! Among external candidates, my first choice had been Jamie Dimon, who was then between jobs after being fired by Sandy Weill from Citigroup. When I first met Jamie, after he was recommended by my good friend Greg Laetsch, it was clear he was passionate about our culture and values. He knew all the old Home Depot stories—including the one about the guy who returned a set of tires, an item we didn't sell in our stores, and received a cash refund, no questions asked. And he understood the values that informed them—the commitment to outstanding service. Jamie and I had an immediate connection, and he was intrigued by the opportunity. Our conversations went on for about six months, and I had the full support of my cofounders, Bernie Marcus and Ken Langone. But in the end, to my disappointment, Jamie decided that the move into retail was just too big a leap. Finance was his natural habitat.

"I love everything that you've done," he told me. "I couldn't feel better about it. But I've invested fifteen years in finance. I can't just walk away." He took a job at Bank One instead, and when Bank One was acquired by JPMorgan Chase a few years later, Jamie would step into the CEO role he holds to this day. I have no doubt that his values—which would have made him such a great leader for The Home Depot—are in large part responsible for the bank weathering the economic storms of 2008 better than most and going on to thrive.

My next choice for a successor was Greg Brenneman, who had run Continental Airlines. His values impressed me. We invited him to join the Home Depot board, and I brought him in to give a presentation to our management team. It was no secret that I was looking for a successor, but I didn't tell anyone that Greg was a candidate. By the time I got back to my desk after his remarks, I must have had a dozen or more emails from team members telling me he would make a perfect CEO.

In the end, however, I was overruled. Instead, the board chose Bob Nardelli, a Jack Welch protégé who had been one of the top three guys at GE. It had been known for many years that when Welch retired, he was going to pick one of those three as his successor. Ken Langone, who was on the GE board and watched the whole drama closely, decided that we needed to snap up one of the people Jack decided against. When Jack chose Jeff Immelt, Ken called Nardelli the moment the news broke and asked him to join The Home Depot.

Nardelli agreed to take the job, albeit somewhat grudgingly. In fact, not long after he came aboard, I picked up a copy of *Fortune* magazine to see a prominent article in which he made it very clear he still wished he'd gotten the GE job and smarted over Welch's choice. "How must that make Home Depot associates feel?" I thought. It's like being married to someone who tells you they really wish they'd married someone else, but since that person was already taken, you'll do. Not a great way to build trust as a leader.

Nardelli was a very profit-minded guy with a reputation for black-belt efficiency. I stayed on as chairman for a few months after he arrived, trying to keep out of his way and be helpful when needed, but it was quickly clear that he wasn't interested in what I had to say. Founders cast a long shadow, colleagues reminded me, trying to soften the blow. I understood that Nardelli wanted to put his own stamp on the company and that it wasn't healthy for the two of us to work together for too long. I was in favor of stepping aside gracefully when the time was right. I just didn't expect to get called before the board and told that the time was now. The politics of how all this happened are unimportant now and any personal disagreements are long forgiven, but from a business perspective, the consequences are instructive.

In the weeks and months following my departure, the phone didn't stop ringing. "Do you have any idea what this guy is doing?" Senior executives at The Home Depot told me that Nardelli was firing our full-time associates and hiring a bunch of part-time people instead. Taking his cues from the grocery industry, he thought he could save money this way. That was alarming. We'd always focused on full-time staff, because we wanted our customers being served by people who were fully trained and committed to the company. We viewed our associates as an investment, not an expense. Even when we did hire part-timers, we gave them full training. After all, our customers weren't going to know one orange-aproned sales associate from another, so every person on the floor needed to represent the company's values and know the products intimately. This wasn't a grocery store. Our customers were looking for expert guidance, not a jar of pickles. But Nardelli didn't see the necessity of training, so he cut back the programs and sent part-time, undertrained associates out to deal with customers. Another change that raised red flags for longtime Home Depot folks was that Nardelli installed HR departments in the stores. We'd never had HR departments because we believed that every manager should see themselves as a "chief culture officer" who was personally responsible for the well-being of the associates on his or her team.

These might seem like inconsequential changes—a simple matter of one management style over another—but they pointed to something more fundamental. The reason The Home Depot hired mostly full-time staff, the reason we invested in training, the reason we made HR everyone's job, was that taking care of our people—our associates and, through them, our customers—was our number one value. We also prided ourselves on making opportunity available to anyone who demonstrated the smarts and commitment to deserve it.

We had VPs and store managers who'd never been to college. Nardelli began emphasizing academic qualifications for management roles, bringing in a flavor of elitism that we'd always deliberately avoided. Another value was entrepreneurialism, which was why we gave our stores a lot of autonomy and encouraged innovation. Nardelli, on the other hand, wanted to streamline and centralize operations for the sake of greater efficiency. No wonder my phone wouldn't stop ringing—our associates had good reason to be worried.

In keeping with his reputation as a turn-around artist, Nardelli was tuning all the dials to save money, cut costs, and increase profits. We'd always focused on adding and building; he was cutting and slashing. The Home Depot was by no means a company in crisis, but did it need to get more efficient? Sure. Any company that grew at the rate we grew, and that emphasized store autonomy and decentralization, was bound to have some inefficiencies. But our success grew directly out of living our values, not out of saving a few bucks here or there. People came to The Home Depot—and came back, again and again— because of our outstanding service and great people. They loved us because we never cut corners on the things that mattered to them. We valued efficiency, but we valued effectiveness more. If having field offices in regions around the country made us more effective at serving our local customers, we'd do it, even though it might have been more efficient to run everything from a centralized office. We knew that if we had ever compromised our values for the sake of efficiency, we would have slowly but surely lost the trust and loyalty of our customers.

Nardelli, however, seemed unaware of the potential downsides of his changes. In the short term, he was able to temporarily increase profits, but I was worried that the cost would be high. It might not be noticed right away, but over the long term, expertise and trust would slowly erode. A few years down the line, it was going to be felt.

Interestingly, Nardelli's mentor, Jack Welch, was more aware of this delicate balance than his protégé. Just a year earlier, Welch had asked me to come in and talk to his whole management team about the importance of service. He felt that he'd engineered and black-belted GE as far as he could go, but they were missing the service mentality. I concurred, having witnessed this firsthand. GE was one of our suppliers, and one of the biggest-selling GE products was light bulbs. Every year, around the end of December, we'd run out of light bulbs. So we'd call up GE and ask for more, and none were available. When we asked why, the managers told us that their inventory levels had to be at their lowest point at year end in order to make their bonuses. They weren't thinking about their customers. They were just trying to manufacture the metrics to improve their compensation. That's the danger of elevating numbers over values. To his credit, Jack recognized this, which was why he brought me in to talk to his management team.

Nardelli clearly didn't have Welch's business instincts. He knew how to "value engineer" a company, as they say, but he failed to recognize and appreciate that we were a values-driven business. We weren't dealing with factories and production lines; we were dealing with people and relationships. The key to our success wasn't the innovative business model, the low prices, or the enormous selection of products we carried. It was our values, and the way that these values energized our people and made our customers happy.

Several years after I left the company, I found myself playing golf at the same course as the CEO of a major competitor. Despite the long-standing rivalry between our respective companies, we were on good terms, and he left me a note letting me know he'd be teeing off and inviting me to meet him on the putting green.

"You know what, Arthur?" He paused, as if about to confess a secret. "I had my people visit hundreds of your stores—not just in North America but in South America as well. We copied everything you did—your merchandise, your design, your pricing, your signage. But what we couldn't copy was your service. As hard as we tried, we couldn't get our people to show up and serve customers like yours did."

I smiled at his revelation, which wasn't really a surprise. We always knew the rival company was trying to copy us, but it never worried us too much because we knew that what they couldn't copy was the secret to our success: our culture, and the values that inspired it. Without those, our competitors could try all they liked to mimic our stores, but the outstanding service would always be missing.

During that conversation, he also told me that he and his team had been delighted when we hired Nardelli. "We threw a party!" he said. Before that move, they'd had no hope of stopping us, but they were smart enough to see that The Home Depot's new CEO was unlikely to foster the values that made the company so successful. They were right. One person can make all the difference in a company. As the old Yiddish expression goes, "A fish rots from the head."

The good news is that my departure and Nardelli's disastrous tenure as CEO weren't the end of the story—for me or for The Home Depot. After five years—during which time profits grew but the stock price plummeted (falling from around $48 a share when I left to a low point of $17 a share), customers' complaints grew louder, and associates left the company in droves—Nardelli was ousted in January 2007 and replaced by Frank Blake. Frank was a Nardelli hire who had come over from GE, but he intuitively understood and appreciated The Home Depot's culture and its values. The first thing he did when he took over? Reach out to Bernie and me.

The company culture, he told me later, "was like a campfire that had been left untended overnight. A big part of the fire had died out, but the embers still glowed." Those embers were our values, kept alive in the hearts of the associates who stuck it out through those difficult years. Frank was able to come in and feed the fire, coaxing those embers into flame once again. In early 2020, under the current CEO, Craig Menear, who has continued to champion the values, The Home Depot's stock hit an all-time high of $247 a share.

The five years between my abrupt departure and Frank's promotion were a dark chapter in the history of The Home Depot. I tried to keep a positive face in public, because I didn't want to hurt the company in any way. Privately, it was like watching someone else take over raising my child and do it badly. For many years, I wished I could rewrite that chapter, but I've come to realize it contained some of the most powerful lessons of my long career in business. It taught me to never take a good company for granted. This parable isn't so much about the politics and personalities as it is about what happens when the values, and thereby the culture, are stripped from a company in the name of the almighty Bottom Line. Even the most successful, beloved brand can lose its luster if the values that animate it are neglected.

Having Values vs. Living Values

Virtually every business today has a set of corporate values that sit alongside its vision and mission statements. But just having values does not make a company values-based. Being values-based means holding the values truly sacred—it means everyone knows them, respects them, lives them, and is guided by them. No important decision is made without first checking it against the values. Nobody is promoted until they demonstrate that they understand and are in alignment with the values. New opportunities—however profitable—are not pursued if they conflict with the values. Values are the heart and soul of a good company. They are not just platitudes on a plaque on the office wall; they are living, breathing standards that guide decision-making for everyone in the business, from top to bottom.

When The Home Depot was about to go public in 1981, we had four stores in Atlanta, and we were getting ready to open up our first stores outside of Georgia, in South Florida.

I remember having lunch with Joe Ellis, a senior retail analyst from Goldman Sachs, who told me bluntly: "You're not going to be successful in South Florida." I was still young and relatively inexperienced in business, and I respected this guy, so I listened. He explained that there was no way we could transfer our culture, which was unique to Atlanta, into those new markets. After that lunch, I sat down with Bernie and told him what Joe had said. He was right in the sense that there was no way Bernie and I could be in all those new stores. There was no way we could personally oversee the tens of thousands of decisions that would need to be made on the ground. But what we could do was to ensure that the people we put in those stores were not there because of their qualifications or their expertise or their impressive résumés; they were there because they understood and lived our values. They "bled orange," as we liked to say. As long as we put the values first in our personnel decisions, these people would be ambassadors for the culture, and Joe Ellis would be proven wrong. And he was—right up until that fateful day when the board hired Bob Nardelli, who could not have been further from bleeding orange, and the culture almost died as a result. It's a lesson I've never forgotten. Values should never be taken for granted, especially when it comes to critical moments like expansions into new markets or leadership transitions.

When it came time to make my own transition out of The

Home Depot, I reflected carefully on the values that drove that company's success and how I might carry those forward into whatever new ventures lay ahead. My businesses and family foundation today are guided by six core values, which grew directly out of the values on which we built The Home Depot:*

1. **PUT PEOPLE FIRST.** People are the heartbeat of a successful enterprise. Happy associates who feel respected, appreciated, and valued will provide great service and make customers happy too.

2. **LISTEN AND RESPOND.** Customers, and the associates who serve them, are a company's greatest source of wisdom. You are not smarter than the people you are serving. Customer needs are golden opportunities that, when creatively addressed, enhance your competitive edge and improve the business environment for everyone.

3. **INCLUDE EVERYONE.** Individual differences—diverse ideas, skills, work styles, life experiences, and backgrounds—make the organization more valuable.

4. **LEAD BY EXAMPLE.** When an individual or a company takes a risk to hold a higher standard and is rewarded by improvements in revenue and reputation, it can give others the courage to do the same.

---

* The Home Depot had eight core values, which were the company's bedrock for all the years I was there and remain essentially unchanged to this day. The Arthur M. Blank Family of Businesses based our six values on the original Home Depot values, with some minor changes to account for the particular nature of our businesses.

5. **INNOVATE CONTINUOUSLY.** Constantly seek new ways to improve results and move above and beyond what seems possible. Demonstrate nonstop reinvention. Do not let unnecessary bureaucracy kill innovation.

6. **GIVE BACK TO OTHERS.** Recognize that the well-being of your business cannot be separated from the well-being of society. Engage every associate in giving back through time, talents, labor, and financial commitment.

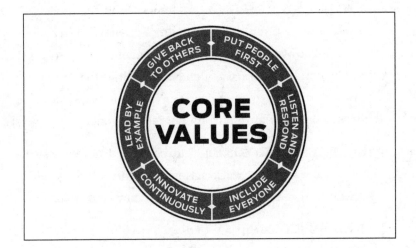

New Opportunities, Old Values

"Well, what are you going to do next?"

The question came from my trusted financial advisor, David Homrich, who'd been managing my investments for more than a decade by the time I left The Home Depot. He knew me better than to imagine I was ready to retire.

"I don't know," I told him honestly, "but I know I'm going to do something. I've been active since I was ten years old. I'm not going to stop now."

It didn't take long for my first new opportunity to show up. In the summer of 2001, I bought a guest ranch in Montana. Some people looked at me like I was crazy. "A dude ranch?" I could hear them thinking. "What do you know about hospitality? Aren't you in the retail business?" But the truth was, I'd always been in the hospitality business. Buying the ranch wasn't a leap at all because the spirit of hospitality is at the heart of the values that built The Home Depot. We always aimed to treat our customers like honored guests and make their visits to our stores memorable for the welcome they received. Sure, I'd never had to manage a cattle operation or deal with the logistics of cabin bookings before, but those were surface differences. At a deeper level, the level that mattered, I knew how to make people feel at home.

Mountain Sky Guest Ranch was a property that my family and I had known and loved for many years and was the setting for some of our most memorable vacations. What made it special wasn't just the beauty of the setting (although Montana's Paradise Valley is truly spectacular, deserving of the name) or the range of activities it offered. It was the warmth and sense of connection that we felt there as a family. We came back, year after year, because it felt like home. We loved the way the ranch treated its associates, the way the associates treated the guests, and the bonds that were created between all of us as we enjoyed that magical place. I'd put out feelers to the owners, the Brutger family, about buying it a couple of years before, but at the time it wasn't for sale. In 2001, they let me know they were reconsidering, and I didn't think twice. I was confident I could improve it and make it successful as a business because the foundational values were already there. To this day, among all our businesses, I consider Mountain Sky to be, in a sense, the purest expression of our values.

My next business move was a much bigger leap and was inspired by a more ambitious vision. I've always been a sports fan, and I'm a great believer in the power of sports to do far more than just entertain fans or make money for team owners. A passion for sports brings people together across lines of class, race, and economic status. Sport creates opportunity, lifting up talented young men and women both on the field and off. A great team can energize a city and boost civic pride. I loved my adopted city, Atlanta, and for several years, I'd had my eye on its NFL team, the Falcons, wondering if I might someday get an opportunity to buy the team. A couple of years before I left The Home Depot, my dear friend John Williams, who knew Rankin Smith, the owner, had encouraged me. "You could probably buy this team for $175 million!" He arranged a meeting with Smith. It didn't start out too well.

"I just want to tell you right now: the team's not for sale."

I hadn't even sat down or shaken Smith's hand when he made that pronouncement.

"That's fine," I told him. "Do you want to have lunch, or would you prefer me to leave now?"

We did have a very pleasant lunch. As I said goodbye, he reiterated his position that the team was not for sale. "But," he added, "if I ever sold it, you'd be a perfect owner."

"Thank you, I appreciate that," I replied. "Good luck with the team."

He certainly needed all the luck he could get. At the time, the Falcons were not an inspiring franchise. They were perennially languishing at the bottom of the standings and playing to a half-empty stadium Sunday after Sunday, year after year. I used to say that in a league of thirty-two teams, they were thirty-sixth. But my gut told me the team could be turned around. Atlanta had the population, it had the passion, and it was in football country. My instinct was that we could make the team the center of a sports-based enterprise that was run on the same principles that made The Home Depot so successful. Not only would we start winning games and make the business side profitable, but more importantly, we could be a community asset, playing a role in the renaissance of Atlanta's downtown and historic Westside neighborhoods, which gave birth to the civil rights movement. Could an NFL franchise be a good company that did well for its people, its fans, and its community? I wanted to prove that it could. And when Rankin Smith passed away in the fall of 1997, it suddenly looked like I might get an opportunity to do so after all.

Smith had five children, and one of his sons, Taylor, took over running the team. The tech entrepreneur John Imlay, who was a minority shareholder and had right of first refusal on buying the team, decided he'd support my bid and introduced me to Taylor. I invited Taylor to a meeting at my home, and he accepted. But when he walked in the door, he echoed his father's words: "The team isn't for sale."

"That's fine," I told him. We had lunch. And he kept meeting with me periodically over the course of several years, while the IRS was valuing his father's estate, always going to great lengths to keep it a secret. Finally, in 2001, John Imlay showed up at my door while he was honeymooning near my home in Hilton Head, South Carolina. Stephanie was upstairs getting ready to go to dinner, but I invited him to sit out on the deck with me for a few minutes and inquired as to the reason for this unexpected visit.

"I'll wait until Stephanie comes down," he said. "She needs to hear this too."

"I have good news and bad news," he said, once Stephanie had joined us. "The good news is that the Falcons are for sale. The bad news is that the Falcons are for sale. Do you still have an interest?"

Back in Atlanta, I met with Taylor again. "I love this city, I love sports, and I love the Falcons," I told him. "I think we could do a good job and do it in a way that honors your family, your father, and the history of the franchise. But what I don't want to do is get into a bidding war with some guy who lives in Chicago or California or anywhere else. So, if you're interested, let's each hire an investment banker and let them figure out what the fair price is." He agreed.

When our respective bankers began negotiating a price, it certainly wasn't $175 million. By the time we got close, it was more than $500 million, and the parties were still not in agreement. Taylor was clearly getting nervous. I decided it was time to step in. The opportunity to own an NFL team doesn't come around too often, and it wasn't a moment to get lost in trying to "win" the deal.

I booked a nice hotel suite and invited Taylor for dinner. Over a very good meal and a bottle of wine, I said to him, "Let's do this deal. We're not that far apart. Let's just split the difference." The resulting number was $545 million.

"Okay, let's do it," he said.

I picked up a cloth napkin, took out a pen, and began to write:

"For Atlanta and the Falcons, $545 million. To the heritage and the tradition, in the past and the future."

"What are you doing?" he asked.

"This is a bond between the two of us," I explained. It was an old tradition from the Home Depot days—when you come to an agreement, you sign a napkin right then and there. And it has to be a cloth one—important deals don't get done on paper napkins.

"But—" Taylor looked flustered. "I've got to go talk to my siblings, and—"

"Taylor, you know and I know that you have the power of attorney. You don't need anyone's permission to make this agreement."

I signed the napkin myself and then handed him the pen. He hesitated a moment longer before scrawling his name.

When I told my team the next day that the deal was done, they were shocked. My trusted financial advisors, David Homrich and Gregg Vickery, along with the bankers we'd hired, had been counseling me not to pay that much. I respected their expertise, but I had faith in the Falcons and in our city, and I felt confident that in the bigger scheme of things, it would pay off. And it has. To this day, that napkin is proudly displayed at the training facility of the Falcons, a team that is now worth almost five times what I paid.

Many people were surprised when I became an NFL owner. Even my brother, Michael, who's known me all my life, and his wife, Carmen, who's known me since my early twenties, said they didn't see that one coming. I'm sure there were those who privately wondered what made the Home Depot guy think he was qualified to suddenly step into a completely different industry. I had a lot to learn, for sure, but I could approach the task the same way I'd always done business: surround myself with the best people, make sure they understand the values, and learn from our customers, who in this case were the fans.

Shortly before the purchase was completed, I went to New York to meet with the NFL commissioner at the time, Paul Tagliabue. He was kind enough to set up a breakfast for me with a fellow team owner—Robert Kraft, whose New England Patriots would go on to win the Super Bowl later that season and dominate the sport in the decade ahead.

"A lot of people are going to tell you that the National Football League is different than The Home Depot," Kraft said. "But I'm going to tell you something else. You pay attention, and the same things that you did at The Home Depot will be successful in the NFL."

His words meant a lot to me. That was how I planned to approach it anyway—I didn't know any other way to do things—but his endorsement gave me confidence. As we finished our breakfast, he added one final piece of advice.

"Here's where the NFL is really different: the media attention. You need to be prepared for the press."

The press? Didn't he realize that I'd been running the second-largest retailer in the world, and the biggest home improvement center in the world? "Don't worry," I said. "I'm accustomed to media attention."

He smiled and kind of winked at me, as if to say, "You'll see," in the way one might with a child who thinks he knows more than he does. Well, he was right. As I would soon discover, nothing could have prepared me for the glaring spotlight of the NFL.

He was right about the values as well. There were many things about the NFL that were foreign to me—dealing with coaches; understanding salary cap, the draft, and free agency; negotiating media contracts and sponsorship deals; dealing with the league and the players' union. I felt like a junior senator for a while and was grateful to all the veterans who offered guidance, encouragement, and opportunities to learn. But beneath the surface differences, a business is a business and people are people. The values that make a retailer a good company can make a football team a good company.

In fact, one of the things I've come to love about owning a team is the unique relationship between fans and the franchise. I'd always run The Home Depot on the principle of cultivating customer loyalty over the long term and making our customers feel like family. Fans take that one step further. They literally feel as though they own the team and they play a role in its wins and losses. And it's true, they do. It's Atlanta's team, not mine—I'm just a custodian. Sports may be a business, but it's a business that's firmly built on relationships rather than on transactions. And that's my kind of business.

Today, almost two decades after I signed that napkin, the Falcons are one of a family of businesses that share our values like siblings share DNA. They may look completely different, but when you walk into those businesses, they feel the same. In fact, we use many of the same training materials for staff in our retail stores that we use for frontline associates at the stadium or the ranches. The name of the training sums up the essence of our ethos: "Welcome Home." We've had hospitality associates from the ranches come and train our game-day staff in Atlanta. When we gather our executive leadership team, the GM of the football team might be sitting next to the head of our foundation, or the ranch manager beside the president of our golf retail business. There will be about thirty people around that table, some of whom lead specific businesses, others whose roles serve multiple businesses. And the conversation will range freely from salary cap to stadium security, from conservation initiatives to the design of a concession stand, from golf club sales to season ticket pricing. What amazes me every time is how the values unite us and how the specifics of each business fade into the background as our common guiding principles allow us to work together on all of them.

Recently in one such meeting, I found myself echoing my mother's favorite phrase: "It's the principle of the thing." A proposal was on the table for a new joint venture that would get us into the fast-growing and lucrative world of esports. There were a lot of reasons this made sense for us as an organization—besides the business opportunity, it offered a way to engage young people, an audience that is often missing from the NFL, and learn more about what mattered to them and how that might inform our future. It would give us a window into how the world of sports is evolving and how we might need to adapt. My team had been developing this proposal for a while, and the deal was all but done, with letters of understanding in place. This was supposed to be the final "gut check" meeting, and they had invited an industry expert to give an impressive presentation, full of statistics and stories. On one slide was a picture that represented the demographic this venture would allow us to reach. It showed a twelve- or thirteen-year-old boy sitting in front of a computer. This kid practiced video games ten hours a day and he had won an incredible amount of money—several hundred thousand dollars.

I sat through the rest of the presentation quietly. There was no question that the venture was a great opportunity for us. But I couldn't get the picture of that kid out of my head. It just didn't square with our values. I'm not against technology, but this didn't feel right. After the presenters left, I looked around at my team.

"I'm sorry, I know you've worked hard on this, and it's a great opportunity. But it's the principle of the thing. Maybe I'm just being old-fashioned, but I don't want to own a business that is going to encourage a twelve-year-old to spend all day in front of a computer rather than being outside, breathing fresh air, playing actual sports with other kids. We're about connecting people to each other, not to their devices."

I could see they all got it—even though they'd worked hard on the venture and were disappointed. No one could really argue. Our values have to come first.

Innovation, flexibility, creativity—these are the lifeblood of any successful business. If you don't see around corners, change with the times, and take the risk to try new things, you won't last long. But values are the bones of a good company— the one thing that doesn't fundamentally change. Sure, we tweak the wording or the presentation, but essentially the values in which we train our associates today are the same ones in which we trained Home Depot associates. If you don't believe me, check out the training video we use to this day with all the associates in our stadium, our teams, our retail stores, our foundation, and our hospitality business. Half of the material is a much younger version of me wearing an orange apron. And the older version of me just finishes his sentences.

You can't reinforce these messages enough. Sure, you'll see that "here we go again" look on some people's faces when you get up at the town hall meeting or the training session and repeat the same core principles. But there's value in that. Bernie and I used to say, "We're not in the entertainment business." There was no flavor of the month. We weren't one of those companies that had a shiny new mission statement every year. We'd laugh when we went into our competitors' stores and saw those things hanging on the wall. Our core values never changed. They were the heart and soul of our company. We looked for new ways to reinforce, document, and demonstrate those same messages, but the messages themselves remained the same. They were never diluted. We repeated the same campaign for decades. Why? Because it worked.

As a company grows, it's the solidity of those values that allows for innovation and agility in every other aspect of the business. In a small startup, when you're all working out of the same room, it's fairly easy to keep tabs on what people are doing and whether it lines up with your mission. I used to walk every aisle of our first store on a daily basis, checking in with every associate and many of the customers too. But as a company grows and there are more associates than you can possibly manage directly, the value system is what keeps everything aligned. Thousands of decisions are being made every day, and people need a touchpoint for those decisions. Sometimes a leader has to step in with a reminder, as I did in the case of the esports venture. But for the most part, when the values are living throughout the organization, they will keep everything on track. In the moments of truth—when the company's soul is on the line, so to speak—people will do the right thing.

‖‖‖‖‖‖‖‖‖‖

Chapter 3

You're Only as Good as Your People

I don't know what your destiny will be. . . . But I know one thing: the only ones among you who will be really happy are those who have sought and found how to serve.

—ALBERT SCHWEITZER

Who's most important—the customers or the associates?

This question was the focus of a recurring argument I used to have with my Home Depot cofounder Bernie Marcus.

Bernie would always say, "The customers! Without the customers we're nothing!"

I'd disagree. "The associates are most important, because they serve the customers!"

Back and forth we'd go, often playing out this good-natured debate live at company gatherings. It set a positive example for people to see us openly disagree. But in truth, we knew, and our people did too, that this particular argument wasn't really a disagreement at all—it was a false dichotomy. Bernie and I were both right.

In the Home Depot model, the associates and the customers couldn't really be separated. Without the associates providing such outstanding service, we would never have attracted such a huge and loyal customer community, but without the customers, we would never have been able to provide meaningful employment to our hundreds of thousands of associates. So customers and associates are equally important. But for argument's sake, if forced to choose, I'd still take the same position. You can have the most idealistic intentions about serving your customers, but if you don't treat your associates well, they won't follow through on those intentions. As the organizational consultant Simon Sinek insightfully points out, "Customers will never love a company until the employees love it first."[1]

Associates who don't feel respected, valued, well-compensated, appreciated, and acknowledged are unlikely to provide great service. That's why the number one value in all my businesses is "Put People First." Treat your associates as if they are the most important part of your business—because they are. Hire people who have talent and integrity. Then consider it your job to nurture them and inspire their loyalty. Pay them fairly—think of associates' salaries not as an expense but as an investment. At The Home Depot, we also gave all our early associates stock options so they were literally invested in the company. Listen to them, and treat them with respect and sensitivity. Check your own ego at the door, and make your people feel like they are valued and needed. Invest time and resources in developing their skills and advancing their careers. Do everything within your power to make them feel happy, fulfilled, and engaged at work. People are the heartbeat of a successful enterprise.

The Inverted Pyramid

You may have noticed that I don't use the term *employee*. In all of our Arthur M. Blank Family of Businesses today, just as we did at The Home Depot, we call everyone an "associate," whether they're an accountant, a salesperson, a coach, a wrangler, or a quarterback. The term implies partnership and connection, a horizontal relationship rather than a vertical one. It's an acknowledgment that we're all in this together and that every person is a key player in the organization—the living, breathing expression of the values that we stand for. They are the ones who articulate our values, through their behavior as well as their words. I am proud to be associated with each and every one of them.

In keeping with this philosophy, we operate on an inverted pyramid management structure. This means that if you were to draw the structure of the organization as a chart, the company's executives are not at the top, as they would be in a traditional org chart; they are at the bottom. At the top of the chart are the associates who are interacting directly with customers—the men and women on the store floor, the service staff at the ranch, the gate staff and concession stand operators in our stadium. They are the most important people in the company because they are the closest to the people we serve. They have the most difficult jobs, and the most critical. They set the tone of the organization, every day, and their attitude will shape the customers' experience more than any other factor.

At The Home Depot, our army of orange-aproned associates was absolutely essential to our success. When we entered the market in 1979, we were offering a new kind of retail experience. This was not your neighborhood hardware store, with its ten aisles and limited selection of products. Our stores were the size of football fields, stacked floor to ceiling with a vast selection of merchandise. So we knew that when folks walked through our doors, they might feel a little intimidated. If you're not well-versed in home improvement or remodeling work, of course the place is going to feel daunting. What our associates took to heart was their role not as salespeople but as guides available to provide expert service and support. We reinforced this role in countless small ways. We flooded the floor with associates, so that no customer would wander around lost for long before encountering a friendly face. Our aisles were not numbered, so that an associate couldn't just tell a customer, "Go to Aisle 3"; they had to actually walk with the customer and show them where to find what they needed. Associates running Home Depot store departments were experts in plumbing, finish work, landscaping, construction, and other areas of home improvement. They helped customers identify what they truly needed—even if it cost less than the item they might have come looking for. If someone didn't need solid hardwood flooring or fancy paint, they told them so. None of our associates worked on commission, so they were not incentivized to oversell. We take the same approach in our golf retail business today. Our fitters and salespeople are taught that they're not in the sales business; they're in the business of trying to help people understand the game of golf, be the best they can be, and look good while they're doing it.

I think of each of our businesses as being like the stage in a theater. The curtains are pulled back and there's a wonderful setting, but nothing really happens until the actors come onstage. It's those human beings who make the evening memorable by creating a bond with the audience. In the same way, a store is just the setting where customers would wander around aimlessly if it weren't for the associates who appear in the aisles and make the act of shopping enjoyable. Even the beauty of our ranch in Montana is not the same without the associates. If a guest goes for a hike and gets lost, or gets on a horse and feels unsafe, they're not going to feel uplifted by their visit. It's our associates who make those experiences special, allowing guests to relax and enjoy the natural beauty and the various activities. Unlike many ranches, which enforce clear boundaries between staff and guests, we encourage our associates to mingle with the visiting families. Our guests love the fact that they can have a drink in the saloon with the chef and pick his brains about the dinner menu, and Dance Night comes alive when the staff show up.

The primacy of service associates is something that needs to be communicated in tangible ways throughout the organization. The Home Depot had a policy that everyone who worked for the company—including executives—had to start out on the floor of the stores. When we hired a banker named Carol Tomé in 1995 as treasurer, she was good with numbers but had no sense of our business.

"Carol," I told her, "there is no limit to how high you can go here—but you have to start on the floor."

She was taken aback at first, but we gave her an apron, and she began working in the stores, in every single department. She even worked nights and weekends, learning about the company and its people from the ground up. Carol eventually became CFO, serving in that role for almost twenty years. She had a front seat to the Nardelli fiasco and was instrumental in helping Frank Blake reassert the value of service and return the company's management pyramid to its original inverted form. Throughout her tenure, she made a point of going back to the stores and tying on an apron, often on a weekly basis. She jokes that she tried to stay out of Plumbing and Electrical but she was great in the Garden department. One day, a customer was buying a wheelbarrow but was worried about getting it home by herself, so Carol helped her load it into her car, followed her home, and helped her unload it. The customer was so grateful she wrote a thank-you letter to the store, but she never realized that the person helping her was the company's CFO. Carol, who retired in 2019, is still very proud of her collection of orange aprons. And she didn't stay retired for long. In March 2020, she accepted the role of CEO at UPS, where I have no doubt she will be an outstanding leader.

Like Carol, Bernie and I took any opportunity to go to the stores, tie on an apron, and walk the floors, learning from the customers and the experts who served them every day. Our main office in Atlanta was not called the headquarters; it was called the Store Support Center because that's how we viewed management, including ourselves. Our current retail business, PGA TOUR Superstore, continues this tradition. Management is there to do whatever they can to support the associates in the stores so that they can do what they do best: serve our customers.

One of my greatest sources of pride is that my children have taken up this attitude and made it their own. Take my youngest daughter, Kylie, for example. She's been visiting Mountain Sky Guest Ranch since she was in the womb. She loves the place more than anyone in the family. But if you ask her about her aspirations, she won't tell you she intends to run the ranch one day, like you might expect from the owner's daughter. No, she'll tell you she wants to be one of the service staff. She's been working there every summer for years—making beds, cleaning toilets, and taking care of guests, who are often surprised when they learn her last name. She couldn't wait till she was finally old enough to move out of our home and sleep in the staff quarters. I could tell similar stories about my other kids. My youngest son, Max, who wants to work as an NFL scout and eventually go into management, has interned with the Falcons, organizing equipment, cleaning up the locker rooms, and doing laundry every day of training camp. My son Josh has dedicated himself to learning the soccer business from the ground up, becoming Atlanta United's third hire and doing whatever was needed to get the new franchise on its feet. I hope each of them will go as high as they want on their chosen career paths, knowing that they've built a solid foundation by starting on the ground floor.

A Hard-Learned Lesson

You're only as good as your people. I learned this lesson very early in the Home Depot story. In 1984, we had a handful of stores in Atlanta and South Florida, and they were a great success. We were looking to expand, as fast as possible, and had purchased land to build new stores in California. We were also considering other markets, and when an opportunity came up to buy a Plano, Texas–based chain of hardware stores, we decided it would be a good move. Bowater Home Centers had nine big-box stores that had been closely modeled on our own stores. They were nowhere near as successful, but we figured that they could launch us into new markets and we could make the necessary improvements on the go.

This plan soon ran into some difficulties. The Bowater stores might have looked like Home Depot stores—albeit rather old and run-down versions—but they didn't *feel* like Home Depot stores. The welcoming energy that meets you when you step across our threshold, the contagious enthusiasm of our associates—these were nowhere to be found at Bowater Home Centers. Immediately, we had to send some of our best people from Atlanta and Florida to help transform our newly acquired stores. Changing and updating the stores' merchandise was an enormous task in and of itself, but changing and updating the stores' cultures proved to be a far greater challenge. It's hard to change a tire when the car is already driving down the road at fifty miles per hour.

Theirs was a management-heavy culture, and the walls between those in management and those on the floor were both physical and metaphorical. At The Home Depot, managers spend their time walking the floors—wearing orange aprons, serving customers, resolving issues, taking the pulse of the store. At Bowater, they were holed up in their offices. Our people set about pulling down these walls—in some cases, quite literally. Ron McCaslin, our director of store systems support, actually got into a forklift and demolished the manager's office at one Bowater location to make his point. But no amount of communication, either in the form of dramatic gestures or gentle encouragement, could turn Bowater executives into Home Depot people, and we ended up letting them all go, along with almost 95 percent of their team members. Turning around these stores put an enormous strain on our people and stretched us to our limits. And it taught us a lesson we never forgot: there is nothing to be gained by trying to grow faster than you can train your people to understand and live your values. We were expanding too fast. In fact, we took this lesson so seriously that Bernie and I came to an understanding with the board that we would cap the company's growth at 25 percent new stores per year. As a business owner, sometimes you have to acknowledge the temptation to get ahead of yourself and take steps to protect against it. It's a policy I still follow with my businesses today.

Like many important things in life, training people to truly live and understand your values takes time and can't be rushed. I remember one time when my mother was sick and required a blood transfusion, a painful process that took several hours. I asked the doctor, "Why does it take so long? Can't you speed it up?" He replied, "If I did it any quicker it would kill her." There's only so much change that you can take in a certain time if you want it to stick.

Are We Worthy of Our People's Lives?

Putting people first is about more than just fair pay or good benefits. Here's what it means to me: *Every day we should strive to be worthy of our associates' lives.* Our associates are spending as much as a third of their precious time working in our businesses—time they're not spending with their families, their friends, their loved ones. The question for anyone in management to be asking, therefore, is this: Is this company worthy of that time, that commitment, that life energy? Are we giving them more than just money in exchange for their efforts? Are we giving our associates a sense of meaning and satisfaction? Are we making them feel that they're part of something worthwhile? Are we contributing to their happiness and their purpose?

Happiness at work is something of a novel concept, I know. If you ask most people why they go to work, it's doubtful that you'd hear many say, "Because it makes me happy." People show up at the office to get a paycheck so they can do other things that make them happy in their free time. Unless we're one of the lucky few whose work and creative passions intersect, we don't expect to find happiness, meaning, purpose, or satisfaction in the work itself—as reflected in the perennially depressing statistics on employee engagement. Recent studies have found that as little as one-third of the workforce feels enthusiastic and committed to its employers. According to Gallup's 2017 "State of the American Workplace" report, somewhere between 55 to 80 percent of people relate to their work as something to be endured rather than enjoyed.[2] Considering that the average American will spend ninety thousand hours at work over the course of a lifetime, that's quite a feat of endurance.

This is a sad—and unnecessary—state of affairs. If we're going to spend so much of our lives working, shouldn't that time be energizing, uplifting, and enjoyable? I believe in the Zen philosophy that work should get confused with play. I don't view it as work; I view it as *play with purpose*. Warren Buffett, who has lived nine decades, says that he keeps working because "I'm having a vacation every day. If there was someplace else I wanted to go, I'd go there."[3] My highest aim for all our companies is that our associates feel the same way. Good companies have an opportunity, and a responsibility, to contribute to people's happiness—not just that of their customers but of those who come to work every day as well.

What makes human beings happy? It's a question that's frustrated many great minds throughout history, but according to the Harvard scientists conducting the longest-running happiness study ever undertaken, it has a surprisingly simple answer.[4] The researchers have followed more than a thousand people, some of them for seven or eight decades, including a group of Harvard students and a group of inner-city Boston residents. They have identified several key factors that appear to lead to a happy life.

In the words of the study's director, Dr. Robert Waldinger, whom I recently invited to Atlanta to present to our associates, the lessons of the study "aren't about wealth or fame, or working harder and harder. The clearest message that we get from this seventy-five-year study is this: Good relationships keep us happier and healthier."[5] Social connections are good for individuals and our communities, the quality of those relationships matter, and good relationships protect our bodies and our brains for the long haul of life. Another key finding of the study was that serving others increases happiness and well-being. Participants who practiced giving back to others were six times more likely to be happy and well than those who did not. Both of these insights are profoundly relevant to business today.

Any company, by definition, is made up of relationships— between coworkers, between associates and customers, clients, vendors, partners, and so on. The quality of those relationships can change everything about the experience of doing business, whatever role you play in the company. For almost anyone working within an enterprise, creating deep, abiding relationships helps build a vital sense of camaraderie, of belonging to something that is shared and special, positive and powerful.

This is particularly true in service-oriented businesses, where every day presents opportunities to connect with customers, solve their problems, and make them happy. Every one of our businesses is dependent on having a mutually caring and responsible relationship with the people that we're serving, and that's a real blessing. It might be harder to tap into this kind of happiness if you're working on an assembly line in an auto plant or punching numbers into a computer, but when you're connected to other people and your ability to be successful is dependent on how well you serve them, you're lined up to have a good day, every single day.

Honestly, it's hard to have a bad day when you're truly serving others. Service is uplifting for everybody—both givers and receivers. When a salesperson at one of our PGA TOUR Superstore locations goes out of her way to find the customer exactly the right equipment and show him how to use it, she feels great, and so does the customer. When a vendor in our stadium serves up delicious food at a great price, with a smile, he gets rewarded with a good feeling, and so does the kid eagerly accepting the meal. When a wrangler at our ranch takes a guest on that special ride she's always dreamed of, they share in the joy of the moment. It's those human connections—those moments of touching people's hearts, minds, and spirits—that give our associates the feeling that there's a purpose to what they're doing. Associates who are connected to a business like that aren't thinking, "How much can I extract today from the customers I am serving?" Instead, they're thinking, "How much can I give today to whoever I'm serving?" In this way, it's possible to elevate every transaction, large or small, into an interaction that generates joy for everyone involved.

Our associates feel energized when they come to work in

any of our businesses. We can't control what happens in the rest of their lives—in their homes, their families, their marriages, their hobbies, their vacations. But we can ensure that even if they had a bad night at home, they get to show up at work and feel connected to other people. At the end of the day, they can go home with a smile still lingering on their faces from the satisfaction of a day's work well done. The thousands of people who work in our stadium during a soccer match can't help but be uplifted by the energy of the fans they're serving and the electric atmosphere in the building. If they take even a little of that back to their families, that's a great gift. Happiness generates happiness. Generosity begets generosity. Service inspires service.

Putting people first raises the notion of work and business to a higher plane. Of course, all of our associates understand that a business needs to make money, but they also know that's not all we're doing. They see the impact on customers, they get involved in our community outreach work, they even lead many of our philanthropic initiatives. At the end of the day, they're getting a paycheck, but they're also getting the sense of purpose that comes from knowing that every day they have the opportunity to make someone else's day better. That may sound like a small thing, but as the writer Annie Dillard reminds us, "How we spend our days is, of course, how we spend our lives."[6]

If this all sounds too touchy-feely, let me assure you that it's damn good business sense. The Home Depot had one of the lowest employee turnover rates in retail, which saved us an enormous amount in terms of recruitment and training costs. Ask any business guru about the secrets to success, and sooner or later they'll bring up the topic of *customer retention*. Loyal customers are the engine that drives a successful business. They cost you less in advertising, they spend more money, they are easier to serve, and they are more likely to recommend you to family and friends. Indeed, research by Bain & Company recently estimated that a 5 percent increase in customer retention can increase a company's profitability by an average of 75 percent.[7] And if there's one thing that will keep your customers coming back, it's the connection they feel with your associates.

We all know the difference when we walk into a store or a business and are met by a happy, enthusiastic, helpful person. I firmly believe that The Home Depot owed its phenomenal success, above all, to the fact that people loved coming to our stores and interacting with our associates, and our associates loved serving our customers. The same is true of our businesses today. When asked why they come back to our ranch year after year (and we have a 96 percent return rate), guests always cite the staff as one of the main reasons. People love to connect with people. It makes us happy. And when things make us happy, we want to do them again.

This is especially critical in retail businesses, which are under assault from the rise of online shopping. Why should customers choose to get in a car and drive to a store when they can have whatever they need shipped to their front door overnight? One reason people still do it is for the service. They want advice on the best product for their particular needs. Our golf retail business is expanding—opening new brick-and-mortar stores even as many of our competitors are closing down—because our customers value the training, the expert advice, and the spirit of fun that comes along with every purchase. They could go to our online store, which is very successful, but it accounts for less than 10 percent of that business. The vast majority of our customers still prefer to shop in person. They want to touch the product, try it out, feel how a club sits in their hand or a pair of shoes fit. They appreciate that they can bring in an old set of clubs, and our associates won't try to convince them to buy new ones but will fix up the old set with new grips or new shafts. If stores don't provide that kind of service—if associates are poorly trained, unhelpful, or unfamiliar with the merchandise—those customers will have fewer reasons not to stay home and click "order" instead. There is still opportunity in traditional retail, but only for those companies that know how to put people first.

If you want associates to treat customers well, show them how it feels to be on the receiving end of that treatment. We celebrate our associates who provide outstanding service through our Heroes of Hospitality and Frontline Heroes programs. Heroes of Hospitality—who are often identified by our guests and fans writing to us about the exceptional service they received from a particular associate—have their pictures displayed right outside the owner's suite in the stadium, so I personally see those faces every time I attend an event. For our Frontline Heroes, one way we recognize their efforts and inspire them to do better is to send them to West Creek Ranch in Montana to experience the power of hospitality directly. Yancey Arterburn, who manages our AMB West group, which includes the ranches, is second to none when it comes to pure service delivery, so we task him with giving these associates the time of their lives. They arrive and find their personal favorite snacks and reading materials waiting for them, with a handwritten welcome note. They get to do things they have never done before, like riding a horse. Some have never left Georgia or traveled on a plane. It is a reward for their hard work, but it is also invaluable training. They get to spend a few days immersed in the warm glow of exceptional hospitality, and it's something they will never forget.

Hire People Who Are Overqualified

Not long after The Home Depot went public, I had lunch with Charles Lazarus, the founder of Toys "R" Us, which was at the time the number one toy retailer in the world. I always appreciated the opportunity to learn from those who'd been in business much longer than I had, so I asked him, "What's the most difficult thing I'm going to have to face?"

He said, "The hardest moments are when you have to look at a person who helped you get to $1 billion and realize that person can't help you get to $10 billion."

I took those words to heart, and it's become one of my policies to always overhire for any position we need to fill. I like to find people who on paper appear to be overqualified for the role, because that means they have the capacity to grow with the job for as long as they want to stay with us. This gives us two advantages. First, they'll make better decisions along the way because they have more experience. Second, we'll keep them much longer than we might otherwise do because they will be able to grow with the role. It's very difficult to replace people, and a high turnover is bad for company culture. So much of success in business depends on the people you hire and the people you keep. Sometimes in our businesses people start out with less responsibility or seniority than they're accustomed to, but if we can convince them that we value and respect their knowledge and skills and that the role offers an opportunity for growth, then they're willing to stick around, and in the long run they often end up doing far more than they could have imagined themselves capable of.

There are people still working at The Home Depot today who started out on the floor when I was there. Ann-Marie Campbell was just twenty years old and a recent immigrant from Jamaica when she joined our Miami store in 1985, working as a part-time cashier while attending college. Today, she's EVP of US stores, overseeing nearly two thousand stores and most of the company's four hundred thousand associates. People like Ann-Marie stick with our companies for the long haul because they're given opportunities to grow.

Treat Every Team Member as a Free Agent

In professional sports, players sign contracts for a specified number of years. Once their contract comes to an end, they are considered a free agent, which means that they are at liberty to choose whether to extend their contract or sign a new contract with their current team (should the team want to retain them) or consider other offers. Good players approaching free agency are often courted by multiple teams and treated especially well by their current teams in the hope that they'll stay.

I always tell our team management to treat every player like a free agent, all the time. It doesn't matter if we have them locked into a five-year contract; we should never take them for granted. We've got to earn their desire to be here. The same goes for all our companies. We should remember that every associate could choose to go and dedicate their time, energy, and commitment to someone else's company, and we should strive to give them every reason not to do so. In fact, in the early days at The Home Depot, we didn't even have contracts for our associates. I don't want anybody working for me who doesn't want to be there. Life is short. Our job is to create an environment where they feel valued, respected, and appreciated enough that they want to come back—not because of a piece of paper but because of how it makes them feel.

If you can create a sense of happiness, meaning, and purpose for your associates on a daily basis, I can assure you that they will be more than engaged. They'll feel proud to work for the company; they'll go home and tell their family, friends, and neighbors what a great company it is. You'll gain customers, and those customers will come back again and again. Put people first, and all the success you could hope for will follow.

Chapter 4

〰〰〰〰〰〰〰

The Best Think Tank Any Company Could Ask For

It is the province of knowledge to speak. And it is the privilege of wisdom to listen.

—OLIVER WENDELL HOLMES

"Mr. Blank, we sit up here in the front. The players sit in the back."

It was January 2002, my purchase of the Atlanta Falcons was almost completed, and I'd just accompanied the team to an away game in St. Louis. Coming late in a losing season, the game (which we lost) was not of much consequence, and everyone was looking forward to getting home. Clearly, the executive addressing me thought that entering the wrong part of the team plane was the kind of mistake a clueless new NFL owner would make. I was indeed on a steep learning curve— getting my head around a whole new business, feeling out the culture of the organization, and learning that what happens off the field has its own set of rules and plays that are every bit as intricate as those governing the game. As familiar as I was with the sport itself, the business of football was new to me. But when I walked past the coaches and executives and made my way into the rear compartment of the plane, I knew exactly what I was doing.

"Mind if I sit here?"

The players looked surprised to see me back there, but they nodded.

"As you know, I'm going to be the new team owner. Don't worry, I'm not going to try to coach you or start drawing up plays. But I need to know, what can I do for you? What do you need?"

Now they looked really surprised. They were mostly young guys, not long out of college, confident of their abilities to block and tackle but unaccustomed to being asked for their opinions, much less their needs. After a brief hesitation, however, their response was emphatic—and unexpected. What they wanted wasn't more money, a new locker room, different food, better training facilities, or any of the other things I might have predicted.

"You need to fill that building up," one guy told me, to a chorus of agreement from the rest. In the course of that short flight, they described to me how disheartening it was to play to a half-empty stadium, week after week. Even worse, half the fans who did come might be rooting for the other team. When a team plays on their home field, the noise and excitement of the crowd gives them an advantage, but in the Falcons' case, the energy was as flat as the field itself. As a result, the past sixteen games had been "blacked out" locally, meaning that they weren't shown on local TV because the stands were too empty. This didn't help the general apathy among fans. The two most popular teams in Atlanta at the time were the Dallas Cowboys and the Pittsburgh Steelers—because, wouldn't you know it, those games were always shown on TV!

The players weren't exaggerating. I was a season ticket holder myself and had seen the empty stands firsthand. And when I'd had breakfast with Robert Kraft, he'd recalled how the year before, when the Patriots had played the Falcons in Atlanta, he had his back to the field at one point when he heard this huge cheer go up. "Damn," he thought, "the Falcons just scored." But when he turned around, he realized that it was actually his team that had intercepted the ball. The Atlanta crowd was cheering for the team from New England.

By the time the plane touched down, I had a clear sense of my mandate as the Falcons' new owner. Our first goal needed to be a sold-out stadium. For the players, this would generate more energy and motivation to win. For the business, full seats meant more ticket revenue, TV coverage, and food and beverage sales, all of which are critical for the financial health of the enterprise. But beyond all of that, there was a deeper reason why I took up the cause of filling those stands. My reason for buying the Falcons in the first place was not simply to win games or to make money. Both of those were important, but more important was my desire to use the team as a way to create community and opportunity for the city of Atlanta. And if the people of Atlanta were not even coming to games, my vision was dead in the water. So filling that stadium meant a lot to me personally as well. As the players described how their experience would change if the stands were packed with cheering fans, I was also thinking about what it would mean to those fans, and to the city, to have a football team that welcomed them, united them, uplifted them, made them proud, provided jobs, gave back to the community, and boosted the local economy. I didn't yet know how we were going to get there, but we'd figure that out. I thanked each of the players before exiting the plane, knowing that the insight they'd just given me was invaluable.

That one-hour flight was worth a dozen strategy meetings with the team's executives or coaching staff. If you want to know how to make any organization a success, you may not find the best answers from market data experts, expensive consultants, or even from the leadership team. You'll find them by listening to the people who really know, the people on the ground. Their needs are opportunities; their frustrations potential pitfalls. "Listen and Respond": it's one of the core values we practice every day, in all of our businesses. At The Home Depot, that meant listening to the associates who worked on the store floors, and to our customers. At the Falcons, it means listening to the players, the fans, the coaches, and the staff. My first conversation with the players in the back of that plane got the ball rolling. Next we needed to talk to the fans and find out exactly why they weren't coming to games.

You're Not Smarter Than the Customer

I always used to say that The Home Depot's management secrets were very simple. *Number one, we're not that smart. Number two, we know we're not that smart.* So, we learned that we must listen. You don't necessarily need a high IQ to do that. You just need to be a good listener and a good responder, and not try to outwit the customer. We actually did believe—as I do to this day—that the wisdom of many is more important than the wisdom of one. We fundamentally trusted that the people we were serving, if given the chance to express themselves in an honest way, would tell us what they wanted and what they needed. CEOs and other executives often don't believe that. They overrule everyone, thinking they know what's best for the business, the associates, and the customers. In fact, great ideas can and do come from anywhere inside or outside the organization if you give people the opportunity to be heard. And when it comes to understanding the customer, the smartest people are not in the boardroom.

A company's greatest source of knowledge is the people it serves and the associates who are closest to those people. I have the greatest respect for the people who work with me— their capability, their wisdom, their knowledge, and their experience. To take full advantage of this resource, it's critical to create a culture of openness, where associates are unafraid to tell upper management if they see that they're making decisions that adversely affect the customer.

Inside the Falcons management, everyone had an opinion about what we were doing wrong. I heard them out, respectfully, but privately I'd concluded that if these folks hadn't figured it out by now—and some of them had been with the team for decades—they probably didn't have the answers. That's why I started by listening to the players and why we needed to go directly to the fans. In particular, we needed to talk to the fans who were not coming, and find out why.

This, again, was a tactic that went back to The Home Depot. It's nice to talk to satisfied customers, to those who come back again and again, but we always learned the most from the customers who weren't happy. In the early days, Bernie and I would tie on our orange aprons and position ourselves near the doors of our first stores. When we saw someone leaving with a purchase, we'd thank them for shopping. When we saw someone leaving empty-handed, we'd stop them and ask why. Did they not find what they were looking for? Was it out of stock? Was the selection of brands inadequate? Were they overwhelmed by too much choice or confused about which products they needed? Were the prices higher than they'd expected? We wanted to hear their complaints. In fact, as the company grew and we couldn't stand by every door in every store, we instituted a policy that still allowed us to get the feedback we wanted, directly.

In every store, we hung a sign that read, "Are you satisfied? If not, call Ben Hill," followed by a phone number. What our customers didn't realize was that there was no such person. Ben Hill was just a name that our partner Pat Farrah came up with one day when we were driving around town. He saw the words on an exit sign off of I-285 and thought it sounded friendly. But when our switchboard operators heard that name, they knew exactly what it meant: the call had to be routed immediately to either Bernie, Pat, or myself. We would personally listen to every frustrated, angry, or disappointed customer. Whatever their issue, we didn't argue or debate them. We took their complaints to heart, and we'd do whatever we had to do to make it right. And then we'd call up the store manager at the location where the issue occurred. A great outcome of this was that our associates came to live in healthy fear of receiving a "Ben Hill call." After they'd received one or two of those calls from me, Bernie, or Pat, they'd call a store-wide meeting and tell their associates, "We own these customers. We cannot allow anyone to leave the store unhappy. We're in the business of satisfying customers, and we have the full authority to do so." The specter of Ben Hill fostered a sense of heightened responsibility and commitment to outstanding service in each store. But that wasn't the main reason we did it. Bernie, Pat, and I genuinely wanted to hear from those disgruntled customers ourselves, because we knew that their complaints were worth more than the advice of any retail expert we could hire.

When we started listening to the dissatisfied Falcons fans, we found out pretty fast what was keeping them away. It wasn't a mystery; it came down to a few specific things. Fans wanted affordable tickets, accessible parking where they could tail-gate, and a great stadium experience, including food, beverages, service, and so on. And of course, they wanted the team to be competitive. The Falcons hadn't had back-to-back winning seasons in their entire thirty-five-year history.

Priced to Move

Sports may have been a new business arena for me, but selling seats—well, that was retail. And when it came to retail, there was no one better than Dick Sullivan, our chief marketing officer at The Home Depot. So I invited Dick to breakfast one morning. I cut straight to the chase: "I need your help. Our team and our city need a lot of work." I asked him to join the Falcons as EVP of marketing.

"Football? I haven't even been to a game in five years."

"Why not?" I asked.

"I've been too busy opening stores!"

This was not an exaggeration. At that point, The Home Depot was opening a new store every forty-three hours. That's right—more than two hundred stores a year.

"How am I going to help the Falcons?" Dick asked.

"I don't know, but you'll figure it out," I told him. "We know how to sell lumber; we can find a way to sell tickets. We need to create an exceptional experience for our fans—driveway to driveway." Get the right people on board, and they come up with the answers they need. I had no doubt Dick was the right man for the job of filling our half-empty stadium. It was a big ask though: he was in charge of a billion-dollar marketing budget at a huge national company, and I was asking him to come work for a football team. Many would have seen it as a step down. But Dick lived in Atlanta and loved the city like I did. He saw the opportunity not just to make the team a success but to do something great for our city, and he agreed to take on the challenge.

Since retail was what we knew, we approached the half-empty stadium just like we would have approached a store that wasn't doing well. When The Home Depot opened its first store, we were desperate to get people in the door. We knew they'd be impressed once they saw our giant space with its floor-to-ceiling shelves of merchandise and rock-bottom prices. But we needed to convince them to come check us out, so we invested in a two-full-page ad, known as a "double truck," in the *Atlanta Journal-Constitution*. It was to run the day before our grand opening. That day came, and we eagerly bought the paper to see our ad. We flipped through, page after page—and it was nowhere to be found. This was a disaster! The paper had made a mistake, and as a result, almost no one showed up for our grand opening. We were so desperate to lure customers inside that we handed out free money. Literally. We sent our kids out into the parking lot with wads of dollar bills—five hundred in total. But without the ad to get the word out, there weren't many people to give them to.

Business continued to be slow in our first year, and we learned the power of a well-priced sale—thanks in large part to retail genius Pat Farrah. Bernie and I were the faces of The Home Depot, but much of our early success must be credited to Pat's eccentric brilliance. Pat was as wild as his giant Afro hairstyle, velvet suits, and gold chains would lead you to expect, but he also understood retail like no one else. Bernie and I bonded with Pat over his love for merchandise and customer service, and we brought him on as a partner in The Home Depot because we knew he had the magic touch when it came to moving products.

Pat's favorite strategy was to find a special deal on a particular product and put it on sale for barely more than we paid for it. I remember the first time he did this, we thought he was crazy. He insisted we buy three thousand fireplace screens at $33 a piece. Those screens usually retailed for $139, so we had a lot of room to discount and still make a nice profit. What did Pat do? He sold them for $35. We made just two dollars on each of those screens. But we also got something invaluable—we filled our parking lots and our stores with customers eager to score this amazing deal, which sold out in just four days. When we opened our first Florida store, in Fort Lauderdale, I took a page out of Pat's book with a similar ceiling fan promotion. On opening day, as I waited in my orange apron beneath the stacks of fans, we were mobbed. Customers were running to the back of the store, and soon I was on the phone pleading with suppliers for more.

Now, faced not with a half-empty store but a half-empty stadium, Dick and his team applied the same principle. We cut ticket prices. After all, the seats were just sitting empty, so what did we have to lose by selling them cheap? Nothing—and we gained the energy of one more person for every seat we filled. The players didn't care if somebody was paying $300 for a ticket or $30 for a ticket. They just wanted the noise, the emotion, and the support of the fans. We decided to focus on season tickets, since we wanted the commitment of fans for the entire season. This was much easier than single-game sales. We focused on ten thousand empty seats in the upper deck—those were the seats that needed to be "priced to move," as we say in retail.

We put those season tickets on sale for $100, which came to $10 a game, compared to the NFL average of about $50 at the time. We could change the pricing over time, but in the short term I wanted to honor what the players were telling us they needed and get those seats filled as fast as possible. Plus, it was important to us to make the team accessible to the community and get people inside the building. We wanted to see all of Atlanta under our roof, not just those who could afford an overpriced ticket. Personally, I also wanted to let the team, and the fans, know that the new team owner was listening.

I called Commissioner Paul Tagliabue and told him what we were planning on doing. I didn't need his permission—team owners can essentially do whatever they like locally, so long as they abide by the bylaws and the constitution of the league—but I wanted to give him a heads-up, since this was an unusual move. He'd been very supportive when I took over the team, wisely counseling me to focus on the business side of things and let the coaching staff do their job. Now, since I was implementing his advice in ways that might ruffle some feathers, he should know ahead of time.

After I told him my plan, there was silence on the other end of the line. Then Paul just said, "Oh, boy."

Dick was tasked with coming up with a marketing campaign. He decided to have some fun with it. The ad featured a picture of me and a quote, which went something like this: "It cost me $545 million to see the Falcons' season. It's only going to cost you $100."

Once those seats went on sale, it was easier than giving out dollar bills in the parking lot. Fans were getting a deal, and they knew it. We sold out the whole stadium in hours. The players started feeling the support of a full stadium, and the Falcons games were back on TV, which energized the fan base further.

A couple of months later, I had dinner with the commissioner, and he said, "You probably know this, but a lot of owners are really pissed at you."

I did know that. The sports press had gotten wind of the story about how we'd filled our stadium, and they started asking why other owners with empty seats weren't doing the same. Needless to say, the owners weren't too happy about this public pressure. I was sorry that they felt that way. I wasn't trying to alienate them; I was just trying to do the right thing for our franchise and for our fans. During our first year, we saw a 100 percent increase in ticket sales—an NFL record at the time. Soon, we had the franchise's first-ever waiting list for season tickets.

Besides putting season tickets on sale, Dick and the rest of the team worked to improve some of the other key aspects of the fan experience. They conducted numerous focus groups with fans who weren't coming to games, treating the problem in just the same way we'd have approached an underperforming Home Depot store. They asked specific questions: Would you come if there was more parking? Would you come if the team won more games? Would you come if tickets were cheaper? Parking, it turned out, was a particularly sore point—not just because fans needed somewhere to leave their cars but because tailgating is such an essential part of football culture. Without that, many fans didn't see any reason to leave home. One day, just after Dick joined us, I said, "Let's take a walk." Dick looked surprised, but he followed me outside. We spent that whole afternoon walking through every parking lot we could find within a half-mile radius of the Georgia Dome. And then we figured out how to lease or buy those lots, which wasn't hard, as most of the owners were eager to do business with us. We gained a few blisters, but we doubled the amount of available parking all by ourselves in one afternoon. All it took was getting off our asses. We offered parking passes as part of season ticket packages. We worked with the city to get more traffic police around the stadium on game days. For fans who used public transportation, we created Falcons Landing, a venue for pregame entertainment and tailgating.

We tried everything under the sun to show fans that we appreciated their coming to the game. It didn't always work. One time we brought James Brown in to play a free concert at the end of the game. This seemed like a great idea. We'd asked fans if they'd stay for a postgame concert, and they'd said yes. What we'd failed to ask was, would they stay even if we lost the game? We got our butts kicked that night, and by the time James Brown had set up his things and come onstage, there were only a few thousand people left in the building. It was excruciating. We could have brought Elvis back from the dead and it would have made no difference to our bummed-out fans—they just wanted to go home. Lesson learned.

Think Big, Act Small

When you listen to your customers, it's important to pay attention to the specifics. Don't apply generalizations or jump to the conclusion that what worked somewhere else is going to work everywhere. Dick knew this well. Back in the late nineties, he was sent to help lead The Home Depot's Northwest division. His first task was to figure out why we were still only number two in market share in the northwest, when we were number one everywhere else in the country. As part of this investigation, he went to visit a store we'd opened in Anchorage, Alaska, a few years earlier. Eagle Hardware, a local competitor just down the street, was eating our lunch— taking about 60 percent of market share to our 10 percent. We wanted to know what in the heck was going on. Dick gathered all one hundred associates from that store and asked them: "What's the deal with Eagle Hardware? Why are they killing us?"

They said, "Well, Mr. Sullivan, you think we're part of the Lower 48, but we're not. Your people down in Southern California are trying to decide on the merchandise for this store— and they don't understand us."

So Dick asked them, "What do you mean by that?"

They responded with a question: "What's the number one selling item in our store, Mr. Sullivan?"

Dick scrambled. There are tens of thousands of items in a Home Depot store. "Snow blowers? Engine heating blocks? Sidewalk salt?" Wrong, wrong, wrong.

"Guess what sells year-round," they hinted to Dick.

"Sheetrock, paint, plungers, batteries?" Dick was starting to feel like a fool. Finally, he guessed, "Light bulbs. Everyone buys light bulbs the way they do milk, right? Light bulbs?"

He was finally close, but not close enough. "Which light bulbs?"

The answer he was missing was very specific. The best-selling item in Alaska was the full-spectrum daylight light bulb with vitamin D. But would the sun-soaked Home Depot folks in Southern California have ever figured out that for Alaskans the daylight bulb was a household staple of holy reverence? Do you think they understood that Alaskans don't view themselves as "part of the Lower 48"? Hell no. You have to really be in a place, in a community, to understand it. You have to be close to the customer, close enough to listen directly.

The Alaska associates weren't done with Dick yet. They continued. "Mr. Sullivan, there's more. Every October, our competitors take all our business and we basically shut down."

Dick asked them, "Why, for the love of God, is that? What happens in October—the Iditarod?"

They set him straight: "No. Every Alaska resident gets an annual check from the pipeline for about $1,500. So, for a family of five, that's $7500, and guess what? At Eagle Hardware, they give a 10 percent bonus on that check if you buy a new kitchen from them. Meanwhile, what is The Home Depot doing?"

Nada. Except ignoring pipeline check season and vitamin D light bulbs. We quickly changed our game in Alaska based on suggestions from those closest to the customers, and we learned the important lesson that nothing beats truly local knowledge. That's why, to this day, we are constantly listening to our customers and to our associates. Ninety-nine percent of the decisions, at least in our retail businesses, have always been made on the floor of the store. Management are just there to facilitate the decisions. The customers are the experts; we just execute.

In this way, you can run a large company and think big but operate small. They're not necessarily at odds. Big means more offerings, scalability, sustainability, and maximizing value for

all your stakeholders. Small means you're building relationships in your communities, giving customers one-to-one service, and tailoring your offerings to local needs.

The Smartest People Are Not in the Boardroom

When I first bought the Falcons, many people suggested that
I find an expert mentor, someone who knew the professional
sports business better than I did. After all, they reminded
me, it was a very different business than home improvement.
But while I benefited tremendously from the counsel of many
NFL veterans, I always felt that my most important mentors
were the fans themselves. They were the ones I learned the
most from. It amazes me how companies will spend vast sums
of money on external consultants, coaches, retail psycholo-
gists, market research firms, and so on, and they'll spend vast
amounts of time sitting around a table in a boardroom trying
to figure out the best strategies for growth, but they'll neglect
to listen to their customers and to the people in their organization who most directly interact with customers.

One of the strategies we employ in all our businesses is what
we call "skip level meetings." Instead of just meeting with their
direct reports, leaders skip down a level or two and have lunch
with people they wouldn't normally work directly with. I do
this myself, and every time I do it, my knowledge of that particular business gets much deeper than it would if I just sat at
my desk and read the reports that get sent up to me. Those reports are packaged, filtered, and prepared. They don't contain
the raw truths I get when I walk the PGA TOUR Superstore
floors, or sit down with the ranch's housekeeping staff, or have

lunch with the players. Too often, leaders are shielded from those kinds of truths, and sometimes they prefer it that way. You have to want to hear what your associates have to say, or you can be sure they won't tell you.

As a bonus, the fact that they are listened to makes both associates and customers feel good. They're not just there to follow orders or to buy your products and services; they're there to add value to the organization. Letting people give voice and life to their ideas creates a culture of inclusion. When you pay attention to what people on the ground want and need, as opposed to following a formula, people feel seen and respected, and they're more likely to come up with creative and novel suggestions. Good ideas come from empowered people. You're encouraging your associates to think independently and to look beyond the scope of their role. And you're making your customers feel like insiders. Of course, those positive feelings only last if the listening leads to change. Listening alone is not enough—you also have to respond. If you listen and then do nothing, that's almost worse than not listening at all. It's insulting. Listening and responding is an expression of respect. The best way to incentivize people to share their ideas is to actually act on them. Associates aren't just looking for a pat on the back or even a financial reward. The greatest recognition is to see their ideas being taken seriously and put into place. If people feel like you're going to listen and respond, they're happy to tell you what's on their minds, and you'll have gotten yourself the best think tank any company could ask for.

||||||||||||||||||

Chapter 5

Going the Extra Two Inches

People will forget what you said, people will forget what you did, but people will never forget how you made them feel.

—MAYA ANGELOU

What difference does two inches make? It turns out, quite a lot. In 2012, we were in the early stages of the most complex and ambitious project we'd ever undertaken: building a new stadium in downtown Atlanta. On this particular day, the task at hand was to choose the stadium seating. Several manufacturers had brought in a selection for our executive team to try out. When I sat down in one particular seat, I noticed immediately that it was more comfortable than the others.

"That's a twenty-one-inch seat," Bill Darden, our project manager, explained. "Those are for your club seating"—the more expensive seats—"and the regular nineteen-inch seats go everywhere else." Our task was to choose one design in each category.

"Why wouldn't we do the twenty-one-inch seats for everyone?" I asked.

"Uh . . . no one does that," one of the consultants said.

I looked around at the team—Rich McKay, the Falcons' president; Mike Egan, our general counsel and a trusted advisor; and Greg Beadles, our EVP of Finance, who's been with the Falcons since 1995. "Try it!" I made each of them sit in the two seats, and no one could argue that the nineteen-inch seat was comfortable. For me, that was the end of the discussion. We would go with the twenty-one-inch seats for everyone because our job is to do everything possible to show our fans how much we appreciate them. Not just the businesspeople buying the club seats but the moms and dads in the upper bowl with their three kids. After all, without them we wouldn't even have a team, let alone a new stadium.

I was keenly aware that the fans who would sit in those seats were making a significant investment to be there. Indeed, as is common in the NFL and other sports leagues, part of the financing for the stadium construction was being raised through the sale of personal seat licenses (PSLs), which means the fans are literally investing in the stadium for the long haul by paying for the right to buy season tickets in a certain seat, year after year. Then, they're buying those tickets; showing up for games; buying food, drinks, and merchandise; and supporting our players with their energy and enthusiasm. For our part, we needed to show our gratitude—to them and to all the millions of people who would be attending other events in our stadium—by giving them the kind of outstanding experience that would make them happy to come back, again and again. You might not think two inches would make that much difference, but I'd sat in both those seats, and I knew that fans would feel it.

My leadership team, who know me well, realized that my mind was made up, so they didn't argue. It was only a few weeks later, when we sat down at the office for our next design meeting, that the full consequences of the choice began to reveal themselves.

"So . . . we did the math on this seating question—"

"That's not a question; it's already decided," I interjected. "Whatever the math says, we'll make it work."

Don't get me wrong, I'm an accountant by training. Math is second nature to me. But there are some moments in business where you don't do the math before making the decision. Why? Because the appreciation you have for your fans, guests, or customers can't be reduced to ROI. It can't always be calculated on a spreadsheet. You have to do the right thing for the right reasons—and then figure out how to make the numbers add up.

In the case of the seating, the numbers were daunting. When you take two inches and multiply it by about fifty thousand—the number of non-club seats in our planned stadium—the result is hundreds of thousands of additional square feet. And we couldn't increase the footprint of the stadium, since our acreage was already limited. We'd decided to build downtown, just a stone's throw away from Atlanta's historic Westside and numerous downtown attractions, with easy access to public transportation. There were many challenges and advantages to this choice, but it meant that our size was constrained. A reasonable compromise, the experts suggested, would have been to reduce the seating capacity by ten thousand or so from our planned seventy-one thousand. Some of our team, who were worried we were overestimating how many seats we could sell, agreed. But I didn't want to compromise on our ability to invite the full diversity of Atlanta into our stadium, and to do that we needed enough seats to be able to offer a full range of price options for the Falcons' PSLs. I was betting on Atlanta—I'd seen it grow enormously in the decades I'd lived there, and I felt the city deserved and would show up for a stadium of this size. This left our architects with a challenge: They essentially had to reengineer the building to get larger in volume—from 1.6 million square feet to 2 million square feet—without increasing in diameter, which meant it had to get taller. Needless to say, this added significantly to the complexity of the design, not to mention the construction costs, but I never had any doubt it was the right thing to do.

The seating choice was important for its own sake, but also because it set the tone for hundreds of decisions we made as the project progressed. It sent a clear message to everyone on the team that we were going to keep the fans first and foremost in our minds during the process of designing and building Mercedes-Benz Stadium. "We own every decision that will be made," I told them. We weren't going to defer to the consultants, and we were never going to do something a certain way just because "this is how other stadiums did it." From the outset, we took our cues not just from our NFL counterparts but from outstanding cultural venues like opera houses, theaters, museums, cathedrals. We took the old adage "Know what business you're in" very seriously. We weren't in the stadium business; we were in the entertainment and hospitality business, and our goal was to completely transform the fan experience. So we hired a top experience designer from Disney. One of the key takeaways from the Disney folks was "purpose over task." They reminded us to always keep our purpose front and center, never letting the mass of day-to-day tasks become the driving force. In other words, put the "why" before the "how."

Whenever we were making decisions, "purpose over task" was an important touchstone.

Above all, we were guided by the fans. This was a challenge for all the international and domestic stadium experts we hired because they were used to being treated like, well, experts. And we were telling them, "No, the fan is the expert. You're just here to execute." We created a 4,500-person "fan council" comprised of dedicated sports fans who volunteered to give us feedback on countless decisions that would affect them on game day.

Atlanta didn't need just another vanilla sports venue. It needed a space that inspired connection, that celebrated the best of the human spirit through architecture, art, and, yes, sports. It needed a gathering place so compelling that people wouldn't think twice about leaving the comfort of their living rooms and their sixty-inch televisions. It also needed development, opportunity, jobs, revitalization—all of which a stadium can catalyze.

Ever since buying the Falcons in 2002, I'd known that a stadium was in my future, but the project didn't officially start until 2010. The Falcons had held a lease with the state-owned Georgia Dome in downtown Atlanta, built in 1992 for the 1996 Summer Olympics. While the seventy-one-thousand-seat venue had a proud history, having hosted two Super Bowls and three NCAA Final Four championships, it no longer met our needs. It would never be suitable for another Super Bowl. And more importantly, we were only tenants within it. We didn't have operating control of the stadium, which was run by a state agency, the Georgia World Congress Center Authority (GWCCA), which meant we couldn't have a hand in every aspect of the experience that our fans would have on game day. And we knew that making fans' visits unforgettable was critical to success, just as it had been at The Home Depot. Experiences are what people remember, long after they forget the specific items they purchased. And it's those memories that bring people back, again and again—that make the difference between a onetime transaction and a loyal and lasting relationship.

There were certain aspects of the Georgia Dome that didn't fit with our values and didn't make our fans feel the way we wanted them to feel. When people would complain about something—the service, the quality of food, the facilities, the long lines—our ability to make it right was limited. When the beer was hot and the hot dogs were cold, fans didn't want to hear that it was not our fault. They just wanted it made right. We listened and did our best to respond, including a major renovation in 2007 to address some of our fans' concerns, but we couldn't tackle problems at their roots. The stadium staff weren't our associates, and we had limited input in their training. We were unable to influence the selection or pricing of the food and drinks sold in the stadium. And the building itself had significant structural limitations for which no amount of surface upgrades could compensate. Plus it would never be suitable for a soccer team, which we were committed to bringing to the city. It was frustrating, to say the least. I felt like I was back at The Home Depot getting endless "Ben Hill calls" but unable to make things right.

Eventually, we decided that the time had come to build our own stadium. We had many meetings with Frank Poe, the executive director of the GWCCA, who proved to be a valuable partner and always shared our vision that the stadium should be a catalyst for revitalization in the community. Naturally, there was some pushback at first from the GWCCA board, but to their credit, they came around to seeing that our proposal was better for the city and the state we all cared about. It was a long negotiation, but finally, we hammered out an agreement.

We'd done exhaustive research on stadium deals in the United States, especially those done in the previous decade, and had come to the conclusion that the best model would be a public-private partnership, which would include a capital contribution from public entities (funded by a hotel/motel tax that had been originally used to build the Georgia Dome), as well as a private contribution from us, from the league, and from our ticket holders. The GWCCA would own the building, but we would manage and operate it, which meant we finally had control over every aspect of the fan experience.

We envisioned a space in which we could express our appreciation for our fans at every level, both seen and unseen. Iconic architecture. A world-class art collection. State-of-the-art engineering. Comfortable seats. Expansive social spaces. Breathtaking views of downtown. Unmatched service. Well-priced, quality food and drinks. Up-to-the-minute technology. Every detail, from the position of a cupholder to the spectacular eight-petaled retractable roof was intended as a thank-you to our fans. We wanted to give Atlanta residents and visitors a place to come together, to connect with their families, friends, and strangers in their shared passion for the game. Do you think that sounds too fanciful for a sports and entertainment venue? Perhaps. But if sport, as some have suggested, is a religion to modern America, then stadiums are its places of worship. We wanted our stadium to inspire awe and to foster human connection like the ancient cathedrals of Europe or the breathtaking temples of Greece and Rome. As far as we were concerned, our fans deserved nothing less.

Who's Paying Your Salary?

Always remember who really makes your business a success. Without your customers, clients, guests, fans, or members, you wouldn't be in business. Never miss an opportunity to let those people know that you appreciate them. Too many companies relate to their customers as resources to be exploited, but if you treat them like that, all you have is a transaction, not a relationship. Don't be surprised if they go to your competitors the moment someone offers them a better deal.

If our players need a reminder about why they should stay around after practice to sign autographs and take photos with the fans, I always tell them, "Without the fans, without their energy, passion, and resources, you're just twenty-two guys playing sandlot football!" One time early in my Falcons ownership, we invited some of the fans to visit the training facility. I asked our coaching staff to move their cars to the outer lot so the fans would be able to park nearer to the building.

The then–head coach was surprised. "That's my spot! The coaches are staying where we always park. Why should we have to move?"

"Because these are the people who pay your salary," I told him. "So you will all move your cars and none of you will park any closer to the building than I do." Then I parked in the farthest spot I could find.

Honoring the fans means showing respect for their investment in the team and never trying to take advantage of them just so the company can profit in the short term. At The Home Depot, we used to tell our associates, "Your job is to sell the customer as little as possible to meet their needs." Bernie loved to tell a story about how one of his golf buddies tried to warn him that our associates were turning away potential business. This friend had gone into the store to buy a $200 faucet, and our associate showed him how to fix his old one for $1.50 instead. Bernie's friend didn't want to give him the name of the associate, because he was afraid we'd fire the guy. Actually, we wanted the name for the opposite reason: we wanted to give that guy a raise! He was doing exactly what we'd trained him to do—taking care of the customer, saving money for the customer, and, in the process, cultivating the customer as a long-term relationship—someone who'd come back to us when he decided it was time to replace his whole kitchen, not just a faucet.

I heard a similar story from my old friend Ron Brill, The Home Depot's first associate, who recently decided it was time to purchase a new set of golf clubs. He headed over to one of our PGA TOUR Superstore locations. Ron knew that he'd get great service and great value there, because PGA TOUR Superstore aspires to be for golfers what The Home Depot is for home-improvement enthusiasts—an unforgettable retail experience. It's the kind of store where an associate can help a customer at the start of her shift and notice that the same customer is still there when she leaves for her lunch break, hours later. We don't just sell golf clubs and apparel—we offer customers personalized fittings using a simulator and guided by an expert fitter to ensure that they buy the clubs best suited to them. We offer lessons and practice facilities. Ron booked a series of lessons with one of our expert fitters.

When I ran into Ron a few days after his visit, he said to me, "You know what, Arthur? The guy at your store just passed up an easy sale of a very expensive set of clubs!" He explained that after his second lesson, he'd picked out one of the best sets of clubs we sell and told the fitter he was ready to buy. But our associate, who had no idea who Ron was, refused to sell them to him. He wanted Ron to complete his lessons, and he was not yet sure those clubs would be the best fit for him, regardless of their price tag.

"Ron," I replied, "you know why I'm proud of that associate, right?"

Laughing, Ron acknowledged that he did. He knew that a great associate would never sell a customer something that wasn't right for them simply to make an easy buck for the company. They're not working on commission, and more importantly, they know that the sales part of the job is secondary; what comes first is creating the right experience for the customer and making sure they feel good about it when they leave the store. They're trained to take the long-term view, to cultivate a relationship with the customer who—over time—will likely spend far more than the cost of that one set of clubs. A transaction is momentary; a relationship is for life.

Of course, you can't take a long-term approach if it bankrupts your company in the short term. This is why I always encourage entrepreneurs to raise more money than they think they need. Take what you think you need, and double it—this will allow you to make the right choices for the long-term good of the customer, which also happen to be the right decisions for the long-term good of your company. The Home Depot burned through half its startup money in the first year. But we still had half left.

One of the things that was unique about The Home Depot was that we made all our important decisions based on the long term. Most public companies cannot afford to do that, but we established enough credibility with Wall Street that we were given that freedom. Bernie and I worked hard to develop a relationship with the investor community in which we were always transparent and honest, particularly when the news was bad. It's long been my philosophy that good news should travel fast, but bad news should travel faster. Many companies try to give their investors the least information possible; we did the opposite. We underpromised and overdelivered. We treated them as partners. Because of this, they trusted us, and most people who invested with us weren't in it for short-term gain. They were going to be there for the life of the company. Because our investors believed in us, they knew that we were making the right long-term decisions, and we weren't just managing earnings from quarter to quarter, or from year to year. But that's a challenge in a public company. In a private company—which all of our businesses are today—you have more freedom to make decisions that may not be the most economically prudent in the short term but are the right thing for the people you are serving in the long term.

In the stadium, there were dozens of decision points where we could have value-engineered this or that feature out of the building in order to save money. But that's generally a short-sighted approach, especially when it comes to things that impact the fan experience. Steve Cannon, the CEO of our for-profit businesses, likes to tease me that I don't know how to spell "value engineer." I intend to keep it that way. I don't ever want it to be said of me that I cut corners at the customer's expense, or at the expense of the community or the environment.

In fact, a good company does the opposite, going out of its way to provide value and to set an example.

Taking the LEED

When it comes to areas like sustainability, inclusion, environmental and social impact, and so on, good companies can make a tremendous difference by setting standards for themselves that exceed their industry's minimum requirements. These things are not boxes to be checked; they are opportunities to show what's possible and to inspire others to do the same. In 1999 The Home Depot decided to set an example by becoming the first hardware chain to require all our lumber to come from sustainable sources. We got a lot of pushback from people within the company and the industry, but we did it regardless because it was the right thing to do and we recognized that our stature in the marketplace would allow us to make a difference. People were concerned that it wasn't economically feasible, but I've always been of the opinion that good economics will follow good decision-making. Today, the standards we set ourselves have become pretty much the norm in America.

When we were building the stadium, we decided to set ourselves an Equal Business Opportunity goal of 31 percent, which means that we intended for at least that percentage of all our contracts to go to minority-owned businesses. This wasn't a number anyone dictated to us; we just felt it was the right thing to do. We ended up exceeding that goal, with 37 percent of contracts awarded to minority-owned businesses.

We also set extremely ambitious sustainability targets because we believed that was the right thing to do and to show our industry and our fans that building sustainably and responsibly is possible for a venue of any type, size, and scale. We chose the U.S. Green Building Council's rating system LEED (Leadership in Energy and Environmental Design), which we'd used when designing our offices in Atlanta.

"We think we can achieve LEED Gold with the stadium," the team told me proudly at one of our earliest meetings. This was an ambitious target—one we'd been proud to meet when building our offices. But this time, I wanted to set the bar even higher.

"I challenge you to go for Platinum—the highest level," I responded.

It took considerable innovation to design and build that level of sustainability into the stadium, and there were significant cost implications without a tangible ROI, but it was worth it to me. With the critical guidance of Scott Jenkins, our stadium GM and one of the founders of the Green Sports Alliance, we succeeded in attaining our LEED Platinum goal in November 2017, becoming the first major stadium in North America to do so. The features that made this possible include four thousand solar panels that generate enough energy to power ten Falcons games or thirteen United matches and stadium-wide LED lighting. From my perspective, one of the most important innovations was a storm water storage system that allows us to capture up to two million gallons on-site, helping to prevent flooding in the nearby Westside neighborhoods. For decades, the Westside has suffered disastrous consequences from storm water runoffs due to its lower elevation than the rest of the city, a situation exacerbated by downtown developments. Homes have been rendered uninhabitable, parks ruined, and health hazards created. Many feared our stadium would add to the problem; we were able to do the opposite.

I'm proud of what we've achieved, and I know our associates are too. It gives them a sense of meaning and purpose to know that they're working for businesses that aren't afraid to take the lead on issues that matter. Their commitment and passion fuel and inspire us to keep doing better. And we still have a lot of work to do. Once we achieved LEED Platinum, we set our sights on a new frontier: waste. It didn't seem right that we'd invest so much in a sustainable building, only to run a less-than-sustainable operation within it. The volume of food and beverages we sell means that large amounts of waste are inevitable. But they don't have to end up in landfills. So we have made a commitment to becoming a zero-waste facility. We're working closely with our suppliers to shift all our food packaging and utensils to recyclable or compostable materials.

One of the most gratifying parts of these initiatives is that we're a big enough player to influence our suppliers to innovate. We can afford to absorb some short-term costs and to invest the time to work closely with our partners. Waste is an enormous problem for our planet, but there are viable ways to avoid polluting our oceans and endangering our fellow creatures. In the short term, they may be more costly or require us to rethink how we operate. But as more and more companies decide to make the shift anyway, because it's the right thing to do, the economics will follow.

There are so many challenges facing our society, our species, and our planet today. But we also have tremendous resources and ingenuity to address them, particularly in the business community. No doubt, irresponsible and short-sighted corporate practices have contributed to many of the problems that confront us. But business may also hold our best hope for solutions. Each company touches the world around it in unique ways, and each of those touchpoints is an opportunity to raise the bar—for the business itself and for its industry. The forces of innovation and competition that drive market capitalism can be harnessed to create new and more sustainable ways of living and working on this planet, and make them more affordable for all. If enough individuals and companies choose to lead by example, industries and cultures will change faster than any of us might imagine was possible.

Pass on the Savings

There are many ways to express appreciation to your customers, but perhaps none better than by keeping prices fair and gross margins small. This was a principle that had been written into the DNA of The Home Depot long before our first store opened. Bernie and I—both newly unemployed after being fired from Handy Dan—would meet at a coffee shop halfway between our homes. On yellow legal pads, we dreamed up our new company. One of our innovations was that we planned to buy all our merchandise directly from manufacturers, saving money by cutting out the middlemen. This meant we could price our products lower, passing on those savings to the customer. Our gross profit margins were projected to be significantly lower than those typical in the industry at the time (29–31 percent as opposed to 42–47 percent). But we intended to compensate for this with huge sales volume—driven by the low prices, wide assortment, and great service.

It was an original—and risky—model. As I scribbled those

numbers on a legal pad, with Bernie encouraging me to increase the "sales" number to make the math add up, I didn't know if it could work. Could we really hit those kinds of numbers? Some of the people we approached early on for funding turned us away out of concern that the model was unrealistic (most famously, Ross Perot, who could have owned 70 percent of The Home Depot for a $2 million initial investment, which would have been worth more than a hundred billion today).

After a slow start (we lost a million dollars in our first year), sales began to pick up. Within a year and a half, our first two stores were doing $25 million in sales. The number I'd somewhat reluctantly written on that yellow legal pad? Nine million. We had blown through our most ambitious revenue dreams, and it only got bigger from there. Why? Because customers knew we weren't trying to exploit them. They knew they'd get incredible service, fair prices, and an uplifting feeling every time they walked into our stores. And so they came back.

That's the real payoff of passing on the savings: customer loyalty. If you can achieve that—if you can earn people's trust and their repeat business to the extent that they actually feel disloyal if they go to a competitor—you won't need to spend so much money on marketing, another savings you can pass on to the customer. Fair prices are kind to customers' wallets, but beyond that, they communicate respect. People know when they're respected, and it makes them want to come back. That respect forges a relationship of trust between them and the business. If, on the other hand, they feel taken for granted—or worse, taken advantage of—they're likely to go elsewhere.

Speaking of taking advantage of customers, you know that feeling when you're at an airport, a movie theater, or a concert venue and you go to buy a simple meal or a carton of popcorn or even just a bottle of water and the price leaves you flabbergasted? In places like that, food and drink seem to cost twice as much as they would anywhere else. And the kicker is, you have no other options—you're stuck there. Which, of course, is precisely why the prices are so high. A captive audience is easy to exploit. So you suck it up and pay $10 for a hot dog or $5 for a bottle of water. Even the people who are taking the money seem embarrassed when they tell you the total. By the time you get to your seat or board your flight, you're feeling pissed off and disrespected. And if you have kids, it's even worse. Multiply those prices by four or five, and they become prohibitive for the average family.

Sports venues are some of the worst offenders in the captive audience game. I remember taking my own kids to a ball game, before the success of The Home Depot, and telling them they could have a bottle of water and a bag of popcorn but they'd have to wait until we got home to eat dinner. Stadiums are renowned for high concession pricing, and the Georgia Dome was no exception when we acquired the team. In fact, the high cost and poor quality of food and beverages were among the many reasons we heard, again and again, for fans not attending games, particularly families and those in lower income brackets. This was not unusual in the NFL. The league's annual Voice of the Fan survey showed that food and beverage had the lowest score among all the factors that made up the game day experience. In 2017, the year before Mercedes-Benz Stadium opened, the NFL fan rating for food and beverage, including value, quality, speed of service, and variety, was just 6.2 out of 10, and on value alone the rating was a miserable 5 out of 10.

This situation conflicted with our values, but as long as we were playing at the Georgia Dome, it was beyond our control. When we started envisioning the new stadium, I was determined to do things differently. Once again, our fans would already be making a huge investment in the team and the new stadium. Seat licenses and season tickets aren't cheap, and when fans buy them, they're letting you know they'll be with you for the long haul, win or lose. For a stadium operator, that's critical—it allows you to project over a decade or more and have confidence in your models. Our fans were giving us that commitment and making the effort to come downtown for games and bring their energy and enthusiasm to the team. The least we could do to show them our respect and thank them for their support was to not gouge them at the concession stand.

We decided that changing the food and beverage experience would be the number one way in which we could honor and respect our fans every time they came to a game. As awe-inspiring as the stadium was going to be, people would get used to it. But being treated like human beings, being shown respect for their families and their hard-earned money—that never gets old. So food and beverage represented an amazing opportunity. It's a small percentage of overall revenue for a stadium, but it has an outsized impact on fan experience, ranking third among determinants of game day satisfaction, according to the NFL's Voice of the Fan survey. Every time our fans stepped up to a concession stand and got affordable, quality products with great service, they'd feel our appreciation and be reminded that we were not trying to take advantage of them.

To change what fans encountered at the concession stand, we had to completely change the model. The traditional stadium concession model looks something like this: Stadium operators sell the concession rights to outside vendors. Those concessionaires have to invest in their own equipment and infrastructure, sometimes to the tune of tens of millions of dollars, as well as paying for goods and labor. In return, they get to control the menus, set prices, and hire and train staff. Fifty to sixty percent of their gross revenue goes back to the stadium operator. Their contracts are relatively short, so it's imperative that they keep costs to a minimum and recoup their up-front investment as fast as possible if they are even to be sustainable, let alone profitable. It's little wonder prices skyrocket, staffing levels are low, and service is poor. But stadium owners keep following the same model because they have high fixed costs, and they're looking for every opportunity to bring in revenue, whether it be ticket sales, merchandise, parking, or food and beverage. What they're really doing is passing their costs on to the customers—the fans. And no one questioned the model. At a certain point, it gets downright exploitative—you're just shaking down the fans for a few more bucks because you can.

It also reflects a certain hubris. We should never take our fans for granted or forget that most of those people have great big high-definition televisions back home, where they don't need to sit in traffic, pay for parking, or wait in line for food. They've got a comfortable couch and a fridge in the next room. As our CEO, Steve Cannon, always says, "Our competition is the living room." It's arrogance on the part of the industry to underestimate that competition. If we want our fans to choose us above the convenience of their own homes, we need to find new ways to earn that loyalty.

As the stadium began to take shape, we considered various options for transforming the food and beverage experience our fans would one day find within its walls. Some people thought we should just work with a vendor to improve quality and selection and not worry about pricing. Others suggested that we should just try to lower prices and keep everything else the same. Or lower prices at certain times—a kind of happy hour model—but raise them for peak periods. From the fans' perspective, however, we needed to tackle price, quality, *and* service. And to do this, we would need to get much more deeply involved with the food and beverage program ourselves.

This was a daunting prospect, however, since we had no background in the restaurant management business. It quickly became clear we needed a partner. So we sought out a concessionaire who was willing to work with us. One candidate clearly emerged: Levy Restaurants, one of the biggest players in the industry. Their CEO, Andy Lansing, agreed with us about the problems with the current model. His company was willing to come in and operate the concessions for a simple management fee, allowing us to set the menus, control the pricing, and train the associates. We would be solely responsible for any capital investments.

When it came to the menu, we reached out to our fans and asked them what they wanted to eat and drink. We invited our fan council to tastings at multiple locations across the city and adjusted flavors and portion sizes based on the feedback we got. Our partners at Levy said they'd never known an organization to hold so many tastings. At this point, we'd also launched our Major League Soccer team, Atlanta United, so we asked the soccer fans too. Turns out soccer fans want a completely different lineup of food—and especially of beer!— than football fans. Our new program would accommodate both palates.

Going back to the Home Depot model of low prices and high volume, we invested heavily in the infrastructure to be able to meet a higher demand. How high? We really didn't know, since there was no precedent for a stadium cutting concession prices in half. The last thing we wanted was long lines. To be on the safe side, we increased cooking capacity by 55 percent and point-of-sale capacity by 65 percent, relative to the old stadium. We adopted whole-dollar pricing to minimize transaction times. We built kitchens at the points of sale, rather than having one centralized kitchen, which meant the food was fresher and ready faster. We made concourses wider to accommodate lines. We created self-service soda and water stations. Our experiment was literally baked into the building.

Because of my experience at The Home Depot, I had a good bit of confidence the math would work out and increased demand would balance out the lower profit margins. Our EVP of Finance, Greg Beadles, shared my view—like me, he's a numbers guy, but he doesn't let the numbers limit his vision, especially when it comes to something he cares about as much as this initiative. But to be honest, even if we had to run it at a loss, I still thought it was the right thing to do. I told my team, "When the competition thinks we're crazy, we'll know we've succeeded."

A Good Problem to Have

We announced the initiative, which we called "fan-first pricing" in May 2016, and it launched in August 2017 when the stadium opened. It included the lowest prices in the league for twelve popular items, including a $5 beer, a $3 pizza slice, a $2 hot dog, and a $2 soda with free unlimited refills (we've since lowered some of these prices even more). The same program would run regardless of the event—not just for Falcons and United games but for special events like college football games, concerts, or the Super Bowl.

Before the launch, I met with the team and made one message clear: *Don't run out of anything.* After all, lower prices are great, but if we run out of beer by the second quarter, that doesn't add up to a great fan experience. We overstocked everything and overstaffed by an estimated 20 percent—just like we'd done for Home Depot store openings back in the old days. You only get one chance to launch a store. You only get one chance to make a first impression.

The good news was, we didn't run out of food. We did, however, run out of ice. Turns out refillable drinks use a phenomenal amount of ice, and when they only cost $2, you sell a lot of them! However, that was the least of our problems. About halfway through the game, I noticed worried-looking associates coming in and out of the suite and hushed conversations taking place in the back.

"What's going on?" I asked. "Are people not buying?"

"Oh no, they're buying. It's the garbage. We can't deal with the volume."

Demand for the new lower-priced offerings was so high that it had completely overwhelmed our waste-removal systems. We had a full-scale crisis on our hands. Falcons president Rich McKay was cursing the day he had personally designed a fancy cardboard tray with the stadium logo on the side—those trays didn't fit in the trash cans and were soon piled high on the concourses. Before long, every able-bodied associate, from the CEO on down, was out on the concourse emptying garbage cans and picking up trash. But they did so in good spirits, because it was a very good problem to have.

The initiative was a huge success. We figured out ways to reduce and manage waste. Most importantly, the fans were thrilled. Falcons and United fans rated each club the highest in the NFL and MLS by wide margins for our food and beverage experience, awarding us the highest scores for quality, price, speed, and variety. Thousands of fans show up two hours early for games in order to enjoy food and drinks, and they are buying 53 percent more volume than they did at the Georgia Dome. When NFL commissioner Roger Goodell attended the first regular-season game after the initiative launched, he looked around the stands with a worried expression. It was almost kickoff time, and there were more empty seats than filled. "Where is everyone?" he asked. He'd been assured this was a sold-out game, but it sure didn't look that way.

I laughed. "They're all out on the concourses, eating and drinking!" Sure enough, as the game got started, the stands filled up with happy, well-fed fans.

At first, other teams weren't happy. "He's messing up the market!" was a refrain we heard more than once. In fact, we were doing the opposite. The market was working—for the company *and* the fans. We did what we knew was right for our communities and the business prospered. Fans spent 16 percent *more* per capita, with volume and satisfaction through the roof. That's one of the secrets of fair pricing—when people don't feel as though they are being taken advantage of, they relax and are actually likely to spend more money, not less. We also improved on other metrics, including arrival experience and security screening, because all the early comers reduced traffic. Our merchandise sales grew by 88 percent over the previous year, because fans had more time to shop. A year after we launched, we lowered prices again. When Mercedes-Benz

Stadium won the bid to host the Super Bowl in 2018, the league's terms stated that they'd be setting concession prices. "We're not agreeing to that," I told my team. "Even if it means they take the game elsewhere, we're sticking with our prices." Happily, the league conceded, and even with our low prices, we broke the Super Bowl record for per-capita spending on food and beverage.

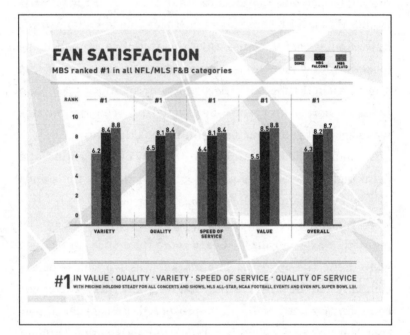

The Mercedes-Benz Stadium food and beverage program was hailed as the "2018 Sports Breakthrough of the Year" by *Sports Business Journal*. Northwestern University's Kellogg Business School, which boasts the world's top marketing MBA program, did a full case study on it. I even received a note from President Obama, who'd seen a television report on the program during a game and wrote to thank me for my "insistence that the food at the stadium be affordable to families." And the best part of all the media attention was that other franchises and even other industries began to take notice. Levy began getting inquiries from other properties to do similar deals, and Andy Lansing is proud to have partnered with us to develop this model, which, as he puts it, "has really revolutionized the industry." I'd always hoped that this "right-sizing of concession pricing," as we call it, wouldn't stop in Atlanta. Although it was initially disruptive to the league, people soon realized we were on to a good thing and began showing up in Atlanta to learn about what we did. To date, more than thirty teams in professional and college football, basketball, baseball, and soccer have implemented some version of lower pricing, some working in partnership with Levy. Other non-sports venues have followed, and we've even shared our data with a national theater chain.

It's gratifying to know we are having an impact nationally, and perhaps even globally. Mercedes-Benz Stadium was always envisioned as much more than a place. We wanted to impact people inside our soaring walls, of course, and our food and beverage experience is one of the most innovative ways we do so. But that wasn't enough. We also wanted to impact those outside—our community, our city, our league, our culture. And when it came to that outside impact, there was nowhere that mattered more to me than the neighborhoods we could see when we looked west out of the stadium's windows.

Chapter 6

Good Companies Make Good Neighbors

*Ultimately, man should not ask what the meaning of his
life is, but rather must recognize that it is he who is asked.
In a word, each man is questioned by life; and he can only
answer to life by answering for his own life; to life he can
only respond by being responsible.*

—Viktor Frankl

The interior of Ebenezer Baptist Church in Atlanta's Sweet
Auburn neighborhood is painted a cheery shade of pink—an
incongruous counterpoint to the weighty words that echo off
its walls day after day.

"If any of you are around when I have to meet my day, I
don't want a long funeral. . . . I'd like somebody to mention that
day that Martin Luther King Jr. tried to give his life serving
others."

It was here in this sanctuary that, two months before his
assassination, Dr. King delivered his final sermon, known
as "The Drum Major Instinct." Several times I have sat in a
plain, hard-backed pew and listened to the recording, which
plays on a loop for visitors to the historic church. The hands
of the clock on the wall are frozen at 10:30 a.m., the time of
Dr. King's funeral, during which the sermon was played at his

widow's request. Everything in this space is paused at April
1968. The tourists and visitors come and go, but the air might
be the same that congregants breathed decades ago. And the
urgency in Dr. King's voice—the voice of someone who knew
death awaited but did not fear it—still rings with as much rele-
vance as it did more than half a century ago.

"I want you to say that I tried to love and serve humanity."

It's a message that transcends race or creed, and it would be
hard to find a more succinct summation of what I believe we
are put on this earth to do.

Although I was not born in Atlanta, I have always felt a
deep kinship with Dr. King, his ideals, and his legacy—as did
many of my forebears. Indeed, there is a rich history of solidarity between the Jewish and black communities. In the early
hours of October 12, 1958, when I was sixteen years old and
still living in New York, fifty sticks of dynamite tore through
the Temple, Atlanta's oldest and most prominent synagogue.
While nobody was injured, the violent act struck fear in the
Jewish community, which had been an active part of Atlanta's
fabric since the city's founding in the mid-nineteenth century.
Though I was not present for this act of terror, I feel tied to it
as part of Atlanta's Jewish community and as a current con-
gregant of the Temple. The Temple's rabbi at the time of the
bombing, Jacob Rothschild, had been instrumental in the civil
rights movement from its start, maintaining a close friendship
with Dr. King and using his pulpit to speak out against racial
injustice and to encourage integration from the day he took
the position in 1947. After the bombing, he spoke out passion-
ately against this attempt to intimidate his people, and her-
alded "a new courage and a new hope."[1] In response to Rabbi
Rothschild's activism, the bond between Atlanta's Jewish and

black communities—one Dr. King described as a unity "born of our common struggle for centuries"—strengthened.[2] For as long as I have been in Atlanta, I have been compelled by that tradition.

What my parents, my grandparents, and my Jewish community taught me was that if one is part of a targeted group, one should always try to make a difference not only for one's own tribe but for others as well. In Judaism, the most important of all the commandments is *tzedakah*, which means giving back to those in need. The term is often translated as "charity," but in fact its root is closer to "justice." Giving back is part of our sacred obligation to create a more just world. This is how my mother taught it to us. She would remind us that everything we achieved in life was a gift, and that we had a responsibility to share it. Even when our family of four lived in a one-bedroom apartment, with barely enough income to get by, she would find ways to give to those in need—helping in the community, supporting neighbors, getting involved with causes she cared about.

I'll not pretend I suffered anything close to the kinds of injustices many of my African American peers suffered and continue to suffer. But I can recognize the obstacles that have kept so many people from experiencing the promises of freedom and equality asserted by our country. I see a glaring example of it right in front of me every day. In recent years, Atlanta has been called "the capital of income inequality"[3] and has been found to have the second-worst economic mobility of any major American city.[4] And one of the most visible symbols of this travesty is found in the very neighborhoods that gave birth to the civil rights movement.

Atlanta's historic Westside was once home to Dr. Mar-

tin Luther King Jr., as well as the civil rights leaders Julian
Bond and C. T. Vivian; Atlanta's first black mayor, Maynard
Jackson; and many other heroes of our time. Once a thriving
middle-class black community, by the time we broke ground on
Mercedes-Benz Stadium in 2014, its population had declined
from fifty thousand in the 1960s to just five or six thousand
residents, even as the city around it had seen a steady population growth. The unemployment rate exceeded 25 percent;
the poverty rate was in excess of 50 percent; over 40 percent of
properties were vacant and/or blighted; and only 6 percent of
children entered kindergarten ready for school. The place that
was once home to visionaries desperately needed vision.

The Arthur M. Blank Family Foundation had been working on the Westside for many years, making investments in
education, green space, health, and other related issues. But
when we decided it was time to build the stadium, I saw a much
greater opportunity to make a difference. From the very beginning of the project, I was determined that the stadium should
be located in the heart of Atlanta, with its primary purpose
being to contribute to the city, and in particular, to catalyze
revitalization of the Westside. There are many ways to love
and serve humanity, all of them important. But one way that
is often overlooked is the act of deliberately doing business in
a neighborhood that needs investment. Good companies uplift
not only their associates and customers but the communities
around them—not as a side effect or an afterthought but because they understand that it is part of their core mission to do
so. As the great rabbi Abraham Joshua Heschel, who marched
arm in arm with Martin Luther King Jr. at Selma, wrote, "In
a free society, some are guilty, but all are responsible."[5] And
the expression of that responsibility, he believed, was "a total

mobilization of heart, intelligence, and wealth for the purpose of love and justice."[6]

Anchoring Change

In the world of urban development, the term *anchor institution* is used to describe a large, often nonprofit organization that takes root in a local community and helps to provide jobs, training, investment, and other resources to those who live in the neighborhood. When a hospital or a university decides to move into a neighborhood, it can be transformational. Once-blighted streets come back to life, new housing developments spring up, people move in, and other businesses are drawn to open their doors. The commitment and investment of a large institution gives others confidence that the neighborhood has a future.

Every good company, large or small, should view itself as an anchor institution. By setting up shop in a particular neighborhood—whether your business is a little corner store, a manufacturing facility, a tech campus, or a giant stadium—you become a citizen of that neighborhood, with an opportunity and a responsibility to catalyze change. Every time we opened a new Home Depot store, we thought about how it could contribute to the neighborhood in which it was located. Of course, we chose some neighborhoods because they were affluent and fast-growing, filled with new homeowners eager to redo their kitchens or patios. But sometimes we'd open stores in locations we knew would not be so profitable, at least in the short term, because we wanted to serve those communities too. Not every play has to be a touchdown—sometimes a first down is enough.

As a brand, we didn't want to be known for only putting stores where high-end construction was taking place or had taken place. That would have conflicted with our values.

I felt the same way about the stadium—it shouldn't be only for the privileged. It should be situated where Atlanta could reach it and where it could reach Atlanta. And that meant downtown. This decision was not popular with everyone, however. The trend at the time was to build stadiums in the suburbs, where land was plentiful, permitting was easy, and community opposition was less intense. Many of my colleagues and advisors felt that this would be a better choice for us too. But it didn't feel right. The Falcons, and our new, as-yet-unnamed soccer club, were Atlanta's teams, and I didn't want them to only be accessible to those able to drive to the suburbs. It would be costlier, slower, and more complicated to build downtown, but it would also give us the opportunity to use the stadium as a catalyst for much-needed change and revitalization in some of Atlanta's most historic yet most disinvested neighborhoods.

We were by no means the only people thinking that way. In 2013, before we even broke ground on the stadium, Walmart took the critical step of opening a store on the Westside, just off of Martin Luther King Jr. Drive, thanks in large part to the efforts of Atlanta resident Rosalind Brewer, then-president and CEO of Sam's Club. It was transformational. Residents no longer had to travel miles for budget-friendly, quality groceries. They had job opportunities locally that didn't require them to take three buses. It was a perfect example of the difference a company can make by moving in to a community that businesses had long neglected. Could our stadium continue that good work?

One of my inspirations for believing that a sports venue

could be a force for good was the story of the East Lake Golf Club. Once the home course of the golf legend Bobby Jones and the host of the 1963 Ryder Cup, East Lake deteriorated dramatically in the sixties and seventies. A low-income public housing development was built adjacent to the club and quickly became a hotbed of drugs, violence, unemployment, and poverty, with a crime rate that was eighteen times the national average.[7] The club fell into disrepair. Wealthy residents fled to the suburbs and joined other clubs. People who lived there at the time still tell stories of how the police would only patrol in pairs, and everyone holed up in their houses after dark. The area was nicknamed "Little Vietnam" because it felt like a war zone. Then, in the mid-nineties, the real estate developer and community leader Tom Cousins, a lifelong member of the blighted golf club, saw an opportunity to purchase and resurrect the club and to use it as a catalyst to transform the community around it. Working with local activists and community residents, he created a foundation and leveraged membership fees to fund the redevelopment of the neighborhood, aided by federal funds.

By all accounts, people were initially suspicious of Cousins and questioned his motives. The predominantly black community was understandably distrustful of this wealthy white guy who wanted to "fix" their neighborhood. But Cousins proved to be sincere in his intentions to uplift the whole community, not just turn a quick profit. Mixed income developments were built, a charter school established, and the golf course renovated. Today, violent crime is down 97 percent from 1995, 100 percent of work-eligible adults receiving public-housing assistance are employed, and the charter school consistently ranks in the top 10 percent of Atlanta public schools, with graduation rates close to 100 percent. It is an extraordinary story of the power of sports, in partnership with the public and private sectors, to catalyze urban renewal.[8] Could our stadium be the catalyst for a similar transformation on the Westside?

Of course, I was well aware that a building in and of itself wouldn't change anything. A stadium is no silver bullet for decades of entrenched, concentrated intergenerational poverty and neglect. America's urban centers are full of sports venues that promised to transform neighborhoods but in reality did little beyond their own walls. Stadiums are "dead assets," sitting empty for weeks at a time when games are not being played. Urban renewal doesn't happen simply as a spillover effect; it must be intentionally fostered. But the construction of a sports venue, a major store, or a business headquarters can provide a powerful impetus for change, if that change is part of the explicit mission of the company in question. As I told city officials when we began the project, our stadium won't change the Westside, but it does give us all a compelling reason to finally sit down and have the necessary conversation about what it will take to make a real difference in those neighborhoods.

In a January 2017 article about the project, the *New York Times* commented, "The stadium's place in that chasm between rich and poor is an uncomfortable reminder of the disconnect between the vast wealth of the N.F.L. and the cities to which they extend open palms."[9] They were right. But that discomfort was precisely the point. We'd chosen that location because we knew we could not build a symbol of what is best about our city and have it stand alongside some of the city's most shameful areas of neglect. We were responsible for making a difference, and if we ever needed a reminder of that responsibility we would see it from our own windows and plazas. In fact, for us, the transformation of the Westside was so integral to our mission that we decided that a key measure of the success of the stadium would be the revitalization of the surrounding neighborhoods.

We really meant it. The mammoth three-year stadium construction project stretched everyone involved to their limits, and then some. Many would say it's the greatest task they've ever undertaken. But as I told my team when we finally opened the doors of Mercedes-Benz Stadium, that was the easy part. The hard part was the work we'd committed to on the Westside. It's an initiative that will take decades, and if we don't get that right, it doesn't matter how magnificent our stadium is, how many games or matches our teams win, or how much our fans love coming to watch them play—the project will be a failure.

No More Promises

How did the historic Westside neighborhoods end up so diminished, even as Atlanta's population and prosperity surged over the past few decades? Many factors combined to create the situation we see today, but ironically, one of the culprits was a stadium. The Georgia Dome, where the Falcons used to play, was erected in 1992. When we studied maps from before and after its construction, it became clear that the Dome had effectively created a concrete barricade cutting off the Westside from downtown and adding to the isolation of the neighborhoods that had begun in the seventies with the construction of new highways. In 2002, heavy rains obliterated sewage systems and wiped out significant swaths of the neighborhood, which have remained in a state of neglect and decay. When the

Georgia Dome was built, it came with many promises to improve the neighborhood, but few were fulfilled. In fact, things got worse. So any proposal for a new stadium that would play a role in revitalizing the Westside would be met with skepticism. We were going to have to work hard and engage honestly with the community if we were to truly find win-win solutions for everyone involved.

When a business decides to engage in a social change initiative, there are three critical stakeholder groups that need to be included: the public sector, the private sector, and the community. The support of each of these constituents is essential if change is to be effective and sustainable, and the outcome must constitute a win for all three. In the public sector, we worked with the mayor and local politicians. In the private sector, we reached out to other businesses and philanthropic organizations. We never wanted this to be just our foundation's project—we wanted to bring in as many partners as possible. Most importantly, we wanted the community to feel fully engaged, heard, and included in every step of the process. As one of the community activists who worked with us put it, "If you're not at the table, you're on the menu." We intended to ensure that the community had not only a seat at the table but a meaningful role. This community element is too often left out in so-called public-private partnerships, and people are engaged only in a token manner, if at all. In any change initiative, if the people you're trying to help are not fully included in the process, you're setting yourself up for a limited impact at best.

To engage the community directly, we went to them. We attended community meetings with neighborhood groups, local politicians, and church congregations. I went to many myself; Falcons president Rich McKay and Family Foundation president Penelope McPhee must have attended hundreds. We walked the streets. We practiced listening and responding, day after day, talking to residents about what they needed, what they feared, what they hoped, and what they aspired to. We didn't want to simply come in and impose our vision on the Westside; we wanted to provide what was actually needed. I'd stop people as we passed on the street, introduce myself, tell them about the stadium and ask them, "What are three things you'd like to see change as a result of this process?"

Such conversations were invaluable. What did people want? The same things you or I would want. They wanted jobs that enabled them to take care of their families. A good education for their kids. A sense of security when they walked down the street. A safe place for their kids to go after school until the parents came home from work. Places to shop locally with fair prices.

What were they afraid of? Being pushed out. The greatest fear we heard was that the stadium would simply spur gentrification of the neighborhood, raising rents, home prices, and property taxes and forcing out longtime residents to make way for new, wealthier white families to move in.

Some people met us with enthusiasm, others with suspicion. I knew all too well how it must look to some—the specter of the wealthy "white savior" swooping in to fix the poor black communities was a tough perception to overcome. The specter of the greedy developer was equally tough. We could move only at the speed of trust, and in these forgotten neighborhoods, trust was very hard-won. It helped that our foundation had already been working on the Westside for years. We had invested in these communities long before the stadium was even contemplated, and that gave us some much-needed credibility. I kept reminding my team, "Let's not make promises. Let's focus on taking meaningful action." These people had been promised too many things that had never materialized. Better to set lower expectations and make good on them than to raise expectations and have people be disappointed. We also committed to transparency in every step of our decision-making process.

For me, a key lesson came in a conversation I had with the late Reverend Cameron Alexander of Antioch Baptist Church, one of the most prominent ministers on the Westside at the time. The first time we went up to visit his church, which was right across from one of the sites we were considering, he met us with considerable skepticism.

"Here's what you need to understand," he told me. "The people who live here, they don't need a bunch of new buildings. We've had so many folks come here over the years and show us plans for condo units or parks. Those are fine, but what we really need is investment in human capital. Our people need education, training, and jobs. They need to believe in themselves and feel a sense of self-worth and self-respect."

His words resonated deeply. "Put People First" was one of our core values, after all. The great Jewish philosopher Maimonides wrote that the highest form of *tzedakah* is the gift that empowers someone to establish and support themselves. I've always felt that the best way to make a sustainable difference is to empower people with opportunity, rather than just giving short-term handouts. It's going to the root of a problem rather than simply treating the symptoms. Yes, sometimes people need money, but they also need a means to earn their own living. From that day on, Reverend Alexander's advice became the guiding principle of our work on the Westside, shaping our priorities for focus and investment. We would work on the *place*—the physical redevelopment of the community through affordable housing, infrastructure, retail, parks, and so on— but our primary emphasis would be on *people*—the human capital of the community.

Working for the Win-Win

Initially, we identified two potential sites for the stadium. The southern of the two, adjacent to the old Georgia Dome, was closer to downtown and easily accessible to public transit, both important considerations. However, this site came with a delicate challenge. It was home to two large, historically black churches. In order to build our stadium, we would need to purchase those buildings and tear them down and the congregations would need to relocate.

For the churches, there was potentially a positive side to our proposition, both buildings being in poor condition and the churches lacking capital for renovations. But needless to say, it was sensitive territory. "Wealthy White Guy Bulldozes Historically Black Churches to Make Way for His Sports Venue" is not the kind of headline I was hoping to feature in. To add to the delicacy of the situation, we would also need to reroute a major thoroughfare—and not just any street, but one named after Martin Luther King Jr. himself.

From the beginning, I told my team, "We're only going to do this if it's a win for everyone. If those congregations don't want to move, we'll choose the other site." There was to be no pressure, no political maneuvering—just honest, transparent conversation. We were willing to pay above market rate to ensure that it was a win for the churches too, but we would do it only if they freely decided to take the deal because they felt it was in their own interest. The last thing I wanted was for the stadium to be built on foundations of resentment and mistrust.

Negotiations went on for some time, and it was an extremely uncomfortable period for everyone involved. The city was pushing for the churches to move and pressuring us to put pressure on them. Time was running out, but I was determined that this decision would not be made under duress. One pastor in particular was balking. He called me one day while I was at Falcons training camp.

"I don't know if I want to do this. The congregation has been here for so many years."

"Okay," I said, "then don't. We don't want you to do this unless you want to do it. If this situation works for you, and this church is meant to be here, and your congregation believes this is in your best interest, then you stay right where you are. We'll go to the north site."

I wasn't playing games; I really meant it. The congregations needed to choose freely and without pressure. So we left them to weigh their options. And in the end, the pastor came back to us pretty fast and agreed to the deal. Today, his congregation has a beautiful new sanctuary not far from the stadium. But had it gone the other way, I'd have accepted that his choice was for the best.

I never want to do business in a community that doesn't feel that our presence will be beneficial. Some years later, when we were trying to build a soccer training facility in DeKalb County, approval for the project came down to a close 5–4 vote by the city council. When my team told me the news, they were clearly just happy we'd finally gotten the approval. I felt quite the opposite. In fact, I didn't know which upset me more—the fact that the city council was so divided or the fact that my team thought this was workable. For me, it needed to be 9–0, or at least 8–1. A community that was so ambivalent about our presence would never be a conducive environment in which to generate value for everyone involved. For multiple reasons, we ended up building elsewhere, and I think that was the best outcome, given the circumstances. No matter how many other advantages the site had, it would not have been the right choice unless it was a win-win. The site we eventually chose was in Marietta, and the training facility has ended up being a catalyst for tremendous redevelopment in the neighborhood.

Investing in Human Capital

In 2013, we hired community development expert Frank Fernandez to lead our efforts on the Westside. Frank has done an extraordinary job, guided every day by what the community told us they need. Do folks here feel safe walking down the street? Do they feel good about where their kids go to school? Do they have access to jobs that will allow them to take care of their families and feel a sense of self-worth and self-respect? We're making progress on all those fronts, but there's so much more to be done.

We took Reverend Alexander's words to heart, and so one of the first, and most important, initiatives we launched, more than three years before construction began, was a jobs-training program we called Westside Works, led by Reverend Howard Beckham, who has ministered on the Westside for twenty-three years. The goal of the program is to provide a path to financial self-sufficiency by helping people get jobs, keep those jobs, and move on to better jobs. Participants can learn soft skills that matter anywhere, as well as hard skills in sectors like construction, IT, healthcare, culinary, and childcare. And we partner with employers to ensure that there is actually a job waiting for them at the end of their training.

Westside Works has been a great success. During construction, the stadium generated more than five hundred living-wage jobs for our trainees and other residents. Once construction was complete, the program filled hundreds of jobs inside the stadium, including culinary positions with our concessionaire partner Levy. As of 2019, our work on the Westside has generated more than seven hundred living-wage jobs, which account for almost $20 million in wages for residents, with a 79 percent retention rate after one year (compared to a national average of 50 percent). Beyond the stadium walls, the momentum continues: in conjunction with many great nonprofit partners, both from within and without the Westside community, we now have helped catalyze and support more than two dozen programs focusing on neighborhood safety, neighborhood development, youth and community programs, parks and green spaces, and educational initiatives, from Head Start and pre-K to financial literacy for adults. Falcons and United players themselves participate in youth programs and outreach between the community and local law enforcement.

We've also partnered closely with the Atlanta Police Foundation to reduce crime and improve safety through initiatives like neighborhood security patrols, security cameras, and officer housing within the neighborhood. Since our work began, crime has fallen by 43 percent, as of 2019. That's a lot—but there's still a lot further to go.

Drive through the Westside today, and you'll hear the sounds of construction everywhere. New housing is going up, old housing is being renovated, streets are being repaved, parks are being created. There are still blighted buildings and people struggling to make ends meet, but it's changing at a good pace. And in the midst of it all, we're working carefully with developers to manage gentrification and welcome new people and development into the neighborhoods without displacing legacy residents and businesses. One initiative that we hope might provide a model for other communities facing similar challenges is an anti-displacement fund that subsidizes legacy residents, of which we're a major funder.

For me, ultimately, it's not about the numbers or the statistics. It's about people like Lloyd Foster, now in his mid-fifties, who was born on the Westside to a family who had lived in Vine City since the thirties. By the mid-nineties, he described his neighborhood as so blighted it was like "living in the midst of nothing." In every direction, derelict homes and boarded-up buildings stretched on for blocks. Around the turn of the millennium, some developers came in, but when the financial crisis hit, they got out fast. His brothers told him to cut his losses and move out, but Lloyd stayed in the house he inherited from his grandmother, still believing that one day the neighborhood would come back to life and prosper. He worked as a tattoo artist, but in his efforts to make ends meet and support his four kids, he also drifted into illegal lines of work. Lloyd came to Westside Works through one of our partners, Integrity Transformations CDC, because he knew he needed to make a change and find a way to make a living that allowed him to spend more time with his kids. After graduating with Westside Works's first class in 2014, Lloyd went to work at the

Mercedes-Benz Stadium construction site, operating a freight elevator. When the stadium opened, he transitioned into a security role. He's less stressed and more available for his family, and the increased pay has even enabled him to begin making some long-desired improvements on his home—a heritage he hopes to pass on to his children.

It's about people like Latia Perry, a fourth-generation resident of English Avenue, whose mom, grandmamma, and great-grandmamma are all still living on the street where she grew up. "My neighborhood was one of the most prosperous and resourceful neighborhoods," she recalls. "It was a very stable environment. We all trusted each other and looked out for each other." She remembers swimming in the creek and block parties with cotton candy for the kids every Friday. And then she watched it deteriorate. A nurse, she went door to door in the neighborhood offering free health services for two years before our Westside Health Collaborative was able to support her work. Now, her vision of the community she remembers as a child is her guiding light as she cares for the elderly residents who also remember those days, and works to generate deeper connections among her old and new neighbors. "We're trying to get back like it was," she says.

It's about people like Cajun, who grew up in an unstable home in a violence-ridden neighborhood. She became homeless after arriving in Atlanta and went to live in a shelter, where she was referred to our programs. To begin with, she lacked confidence in her own capabilities and feared the judgment of other people, but she also had a determination to overcome that mindset and to succeed. "There are so many things I want to learn that I was never taught," she said. Cajun entered the soft-skills program and went on to pursue nursing training, which led her to her dream job as a nurse technician on the cardiac unit at Emory Hospital. She has not only a career position but also full benefits, and Emory is covering 80 percent of her continuing education costs.

Yes! In Our Backyard

Eleven acres of striped pavement. That's the plan that was presented to me for the site of the Georgia Dome, just north of the new stadium. I sat in the construction trailer with our team and listened as they explained the rationale for the giant, single-level parking lot that they had decided would replace the old stadium.

It made sense. We needed parking, and that land was ours to use. But as I tried to picture it, I thought of the Westside residents, who had lived in the shadow of that concrete barricade for so long. Was this much better—to replace it with acres of blacktop that were only used on game days?

"Let's rethink this," I said.

There was dead silence. I could see the team thinking, "Oh, boy, here he goes. . . ."

"Don't worry, I understand that we need parking," I said. "But what I want to find out is, what does the community need for the other three-hundred-plus days when it's sitting empty? How can we create a space that's not just a dead asset?"

So often, companies think one-dimensionally about their own needs. If a company really sees itself as a citizen of the neighborhood, then every asset can be reexamined in light of the question: How else might this be used when we're not using it?

We set out to answer that question, and the result was the green space that's known today as The Home Depot Backyard. On game days and other major events at the stadium, it provides parking and a premium tailgating experience. On all the other days, it's a community park, open to the public and programmed with free activities like music, dance, art, sports, movies, yoga classes, and many other things that the people who live nearby told us they wanted. There are food and drinks available, with the same fan-friendly pricing we use inside the stadium.

When we officially opened the park, Atlanta's mayor, Keisha Lance Bottoms, attended. As she stood up to make her remarks, I saw that she was crying.

"My grandmother had a home—like, right over there," she said, pointing across the Backyard. "And we never had any place to go play."

Choking back her tears, she spoke about how meaningful it was to have this kind of community park where kids could come and play and adults could come and engage in healthy activities together.

In many ways, I'm just as proud of the Backyard as I am of the stadium. Don't get me wrong—the stadium is magnificent, and when people are in it, it's an extraordinary venue for the community to come together. But that doesn't happen every day. The Backyard is available to those who are living right there, in those communities, day in and day out. And when we approached The Home Depot to invite them to sponsor it, it didn't surprise me that they jumped at the chance to connect their brand to something so life-affirming and community-focused. It made me very proud to be able to put the name of the company I cofounded on this eleven-acre almost-parking-lot.

Good Neighbors Inspire Partnership

Our family foundation has invested heavily in the Westside, but more importantly, we've inspired our public and private partners to invest alongside us, multiplying our investment many times over. For example, every corporate sponsor of the stadium committed funds to the Westside. Our role was to get the momentum started and keep it going, and then leverage our influence and relationships to bring others on board. Bill Gates has used the term *catalytic philanthropy* to describe this type of approach, in which well-targeted private funding triggers business and government to play their parts, harnessing both market forces and political will for maximum impact.[10]

To my great satisfaction, our hope that the stadium and our investments in the Westside would be catalytic in this way, attracting more investment and development, is being borne out. The massive Gulch development project, just east of the stadium, will transform a sprawl of sunken railyards and parking lots into millions of square feet of new homes, shops, businesses, and parks. Downtown is thriving. Atlanta's Beltline public trail is now finished to the west of the city. Art galleries and restaurants are opening in Castleberry Hills. The YMCA just moved its Atlanta headquarters to the Westside and opened an early-childhood education center.

Other philanthropists have been inspired as well, as have businesses. When Dan Cathy, CEO of Chick-fil-A, wanted to get involved, I met him for lunch on the Westside.

"What can we do?" he asked.

"Step outside with me," I replied. "Let me show you something." Right down the block from where we were meeting was a KFC, and there was a line of people waiting for their lunch.

"If you want to help the Westside," I proposed, "you could start by opening a store, right here. Your products are better, and your associates are fabulous. Do business in the neighborhood."

Good companies make good neighbors. Chick-fil-A did just as I suggested and opened on the Westside, providing affordable food, jobs, and more to the neighborhood. And Dan has been one of the leading proponents of change on the Westside. Because of examples like his, other companies are increasingly feeling confident that the neighborhood is a safe place to do business.

A strong and healthy forest doesn't thrive because of one tree. We now know that beneath the ground, the root systems of many trees connect and communicate, sharing nutrients and information that helps the whole forest flourish. When I think of a community like the Westside, my hope is that every business, nonprofit, and other institution that takes root there will contribute to the thriving of the whole, bringing people together and encouraging them to support and uplift one another.

Progress, in Perspective

In so many ways, we're making tremendous progress on the Westside—and we have a long way to go. Both are true. As an example, let's take a single statistic: third-grade reading. Since our work began, it's increased 300 percent. That's an incredible gain, by any standard. Look at the numbers from another angle, however, and here's the same story: third-grade reading has increased from 6 percent of students to 18 percent of students. Still progress, but seen in perspective.

One of my personal heroes, whom I'm proud to also call a friend, is Ambassador Andrew Young, a former Georgia congressman and Atlanta mayor, as well as a close confidant to Martin Luther King Jr. I've always felt blessed to spend time with Andy, and one of my most treasured memories is of an Outward Bound trip we once took together with our families. It wasn't easy to convince Andy to come on the trip. When I first invited him, he just laughed.

"I was in the civil rights movement," he told me. "I've been beaten and jailed. My life has been dangerous enough. I don't need to go looking for trouble."

His wife at the time, Jean, had other ideas. She had already taken one trip and had a fantastic time, so she insisted the whole family attend. After a long day of rafting the Chattooga River, we made camp on a rainy night, and Andy and I scrambled together up a muddy bank to find firewood. Later, as we huddled around the campfire trying to get dry, with the rain beating down around us, Andy began to tell stories from his time with Dr. King. He talked about marching at Selma, about trying in vain to reason with Klansmen, about being brutally beaten in Florida. And he told us about that fateful night in April 1968, at a motel in Memphis. Dr. King was in a lighthearted mood, he recalled, starting a pillow fight with his fellow activists. Later, Andy waited for him to come downstairs so they could go out for dinner. "Do I really need a coat?" Dr. King called out from the balcony above. And then a shot rang out. By the time Andy reached him, his friend still had a pulse, but he knew it was too late.

As I listened, captivated, all the minor discomforts of our current circumstances faded out of my awareness. For those few hours, thanks to his masterful storytelling, I felt as though I too had walked alongside the heroes of the civil rights movement.

When we began our work on the Westside, I invited Andy to address our board, knowing that he could set the tone and historical context for the project like none other. We gathered at Paschal's, the legendary soul food restaurant that was one of the first places in the city to defy segregation and serve black and white customers at the same tables. During the civil rights era, Paschal's became the unofficial headquarters of the movement—a venue for strategy sessions, a place to debrief, and a safe haven for activists returning from jail who knew the restaurant would be open to them at any hour of the night. Andy spoke powerfully about his own memories, as well as offering guidance for how we might best approach the communities adjacent to our proposed stadium. And he reminded us that above all, we must have patience and be committed for the long term. With the authority of one who has truly been on the frontlines of a revolution, he emphasized that change comes not all at once but little by little.

Elsewhere, he's expanded on this sentiment. "Everybody is thinking in terms of quarterly results," he told an interviewer in 2010. Citing an old Native American proverb, he said, "You've got to make decisions for the long, long haul—seven generations yet unborn. I'm not concerned for me anymore. It's the world that I'm leaving for my grandchildren and great-grandchildren."[11]

A shift that is truly worthwhile does not happen overnight, or in the time it takes to build a stadium, or even in the course of a single lifetime. But if enough people are committed, it does happen. Any time I find myself feeling discouraged or impatient at the slow pace of progress, I remember Andy's words, and his call for more people to "have the discipline and the commitment and the courage to take on the tough problems."[12] I'm both inspired and humbled by his example as I stand in the beautiful building we created and look out over the Westside, where our work continues.

Chapter 7

▪▪▪▪▪▪▪▪▪▪▪

You Always Get More Than You Give

The measure of your life will not be in what you accumulate,
but in what you give away.

—WAYNE DYER

Somewhere on an open plain in the middle of America, an orange Home Depot truck pulls up to a stoplight, with its right indicator on. Clear skies and an empty road lie in the direction it's headed, but in the other direction, a monster storm is building on the horizon, lightning flashing and clouds gathering. The driver looks both ways. His indicator stops. There's a pregnant pause, and then the left indicator begins to blink.

This was always my favorite Home Depot ad. That brief, simple video perfectly captures what made me most proud of our company. We didn't turn away from problems, disasters, or needs in our communities. We turned toward them, feeling responsible for doing our part to uplift our neighborhoods and put things right. When our competitors raised their prices during Hurricane Andrew, we refused to do so. When essential materials like plywood became scarce, and some suppliers began jacking up their prices, we set a policy that we'd sell them at cost plus freight, making no profit. We also used our leverage to curb price increases on the part of some suppliers. We rerouted our supply chains to get materials to the areas of need and donated supplies and manpower to rebuild homes. We dug people out of ice storms in the Northeast. We donated shovels, masks, gloves, and other supplies to rescue workers after the horrors of the Oklahoma City bombing. We built playgrounds for kids in partnership with Boys & Girls Clubs, and homes with Habitat for Humanity. Among all the accolades the company received over the years, my most cherished was the 2001 Harris Interactive survey in which American consumers ranked us number one in social responsibility.

We didn't do it to burnish our brand or generate business; we did it because it was the right thing to do. But what I've learned, over several decades in philanthropy and business, is that the more you give, the more you get back. Even from a purely economic standpoint, this is true. The people of Florida didn't forget that we maintained our prices and kept our supply chain moving after the hurricane. Nor did the vendors that we continued to pay on time. We're doing the same thing in our businesses right now, as the economy buckles under the effects of the COVID-19 pandemic—continuing to honor our commitments to our partners. In the process, we're earning goodwill and loyalty, and when things look brighter, those same vendors are likely to give us the best deals because they're grateful we stood by them. That's not the reason we do the right thing, but it's a validation of the good business sense in being generous and compassionate during difficult times.

There are few things in life that bring a greater sense of satisfaction and purpose than the act of giving. In this sense, you always get more than you give. And giving is infectious—

the more you do it, the more you want to do it. Throughout my life and my career, I've held giving back to others as one of my core values and I've sought to integrate it into all my businesses. It's not optional; it's essential. I've publicly taken the Giving Pledge—an initiative launched in 2010 by Bill and Melinda Gates to encourage high-net-worth individuals and families to commit to giving away more than half of their wealth within their lifetimes—and committed 95 percent of my wealth to my family foundation. It's what brings meaning to everything I'm doing, and I hope our associates are motivated by knowing that all the value they are creating will get recycled back into society. Our family foundation is not only the beneficiary of our for-profit businesses—as Penny McPhee, who's been president of the foundation since 2004, likes to say, "It's the connective tissue between them." In my mind, it's really all one enterprise.

A Culture of Giving

The spirit of giving isn't just about supporting external causes. Oftentimes, there are people in need right there in your own workplace. When those hurricanes struck, some of the people affected were Home Depot associates. We had men and women working in our stores who told us they didn't know if their houses would still be standing when they got home. Yet they continued to show up to serve their customers and communities, knowing that at a time like that, people needed our stores to be open so they could get the materials to repair the storm damage. We always did our best to support our associates in whatever way we could, but as the company grew, so did the number of people in need—people who'd been knocked sideways by life events they were unprepared for. Bernie and I used to get heart-rending letters. A single mother diagnosed with cancer who couldn't pay medical expenses that were not covered by her insurance. An associate whose family had lost their home in a fire. A man who had lost his father and could not afford the cost of a funeral. A woman who needed open-heart surgery and wouldn't be able to work for several months. As a company, we provided good benefits, but there were always individual cases where people needed more. These people were our family, and we wanted to help. We knew they felt that way about one another as well.

It was out of this desire that the Homer Fund was born. We announced it at the company's twentieth anniversary celebration in 1999. Bernie, Ken, and I each donated $5 million to launch the fund, but the best thing about it was that our associates were invited to donate as well, with every dollar being dedicated to helping their colleagues in times of need. And they did, with a generosity that inspired us all. More than two decades later, a stunning 93 percent of The Home Depot's associates contribute annually to the fund. If you want to know what makes The Home Depot a great company, that number says it all.

The Homer Fund is a true testimony to the power of culture. It isn't just about the company and its founders taking care of its people; it is about the people taking care of one another. They truly feel like a family, and family is where you turn when things get tough. Since its founding, the fund has provided close to $200 million in grants to more than 146,000 associates.

The Meaning Factor

For a company, one of the greatest benefits of being socially responsible, engaged, and generous is the impact it will have on your associates. If you can integrate giving into your business model, it will infuse your workplace with a sense of purpose and meaning that makes your associates proud to work there. It's hard to put a dollar value on that kind of pride, but if I could, it would be a high one. Sure, people like to work for companies that are successful, that pay them well, and that offer great benefits. They like to work for companies that are innovative and attract smart, interesting people. But they love to work for companies that they perceive as truly caring about people and making a difference in the world.

Younger generations in particular are increasingly seeking meaning and purpose as a critical part of their compensation package. Many even say they'd take a pay cut in exchange for those elusive feelings. The San Francisco–based leadership development group BetterUp Labs found that nine out of ten people surveyed would be willing to sacrifice future earnings for work that was meaningful.[1] As the researcher Tammy Erickson puts it in *Harvard Business Review*, "Meaning is the new money."[2] Studies consistently show that employees who find their work meaningful will be more engaged, more productive, and more effective, and they are more likely to stay with the company, reducing turnover and recruitment costs. Good companies understand this and make it a strategic priority.

Some degree of meaning can be derived from the work itself, particularly in service-oriented roles where associates are creating relationships with customers, guests, or fans—providing value and solving problems directly. But inevitably, many of the tasks we undertake as part of our work are routine. This is where a robust engagement with social impact can be transformational for a company. When people feel as though they're part of something that's bigger than they are, that's meaningful. When they feel as though they're contributing, that's meaningful. When they see people's lives changed as a result, that's meaningful. One of the most powerful strategies we've employed—for social impact *and* associate satisfaction—is getting the people who work in every business actively involved with our philanthropic efforts.

Many companies today engage in corporate philanthropy, and that's a very good thing. But it's less common to see companies empower and facilitate a spirit of giving in every associate, building philanthropy into the DNA of their business models. Typically, the decisions about where the money goes are made either by the leaders or by someone in the marketing department. Causes are chosen because they're close to the leader's heart or because they're brand-aligned. Those are not bad reasons to give, but getting the associates involved in the process can radically change the nature of a company's giving, and in the process, transform the culture of the company as a whole. When you do this, the impact is exponential, as I first learned far away from our business and foundation headquarters, on the trails of our Montana ranch.

When I used to visit Mountain Sky as a guest back in the nineties, I met a young wrangler named Tawnya Rupe. She had a wonderful way with horses and a great love for the land. After I bought the ranch and she graduated from college, I was delighted that she stayed on to work for us. I had a feeling that she'd be with us for many years to come. What neither I, nor Tawnya, could have predicted back then was that she would end up managing a philanthropic initiative that would become a model for all our businesses, from the Falcons to Atlanta United to the golf retail stores.

It began soon after I took over the ranch, when I decided to allocate a portion of our foundation's annual budget to Mountain Sky, to be used to support local nonprofits. Montana is a state that is rich in beauty, but it's also one of the poorest per capita in America. My family and I loved the land and wanted to do whatever we could to help the local community. I was concerned, however, that when it came to deciding how to use the funds, our Atlanta-based foundation staff wouldn't know where to start, so I asked the ranch associates to form a committee to help us allocate and manage our giving. Tawnya was part of that first group, along with others whose regular jobs were housekeeping, food preparation, and taking care of the horses and the land. None of them had a background in philanthropy, and many were not long out of school. But they lived and worked in the local communities, and they were in touch with the needs of their neighbors and the natural environment. We tasked them with setting funding priorities, evaluating grant applications, conducting site visits, and monitoring impact. They received some basic training and support from the foundation staff, but the responsibility was in their hands. Nobody would be making the decisions for them.

On my visits to the ranch, I would often take rides with Tawnya, whose responsibilities, besides serving on the new committee and running the ranch's gift shop, included caring for my family's horses. As we made our way along wooded trails and up into the high pastures, I found myself listening in amazement as she told me stories about the committee's work. They'd funded a new ambulance for a local town, after-school programs for kids, and community health initiatives. It was clear that these associates were astute and dedicated to the task—asking deep, thoughtful questions on site visits; listening with compassion and open-mindedness; cultivating key relationships in the communities; and carefully considering the best ways to use the funds for maximum impact. Trained professionals from some other part of the country could not have possibly done such a great job as these folks who cared deeply about the place they live and work. And they loved it. They were volunteering their own time and effort, on top of the long hours they worked at the ranch. I could feel the pride and satisfaction it gave them. Personally, they might not have had the financial means to give, but in their role as stewards of the fund, they were making a difference, and it was changing them as well.

Our head housekeeper at the time, Sally Myers, was a single mother of four. She got involved in our giving program, with a particular focus on families.

"Kids are my thing," she said. She'd lived in the area for thirty years, and she knew all the local family nonprofits intimately—because before coming to work for us, she'd relied on them herself. "Ninety percent of these kids' groups— Boys and Girls Club, Child Care Connections—at one time or another, while raising my four children here, I've used them. I know which ones really help."[3]

Now, Sally found herself in a position of being able to direct funding to those same organizations of which she'd once been a beneficiary—and there was no one more qualified than her to know how to make sure it reached the people who would use it best.

Soon Tawnya took over the role of fund director. I was so inspired by what they'd achieved and the impact it had both on the community and the associates that I decided to roll out a similar program across all the businesses. Many of them already had philanthropic components, such as the Atlanta Falcons Youth Foundation, but they weren't led by the associates in the way the Mountain Sky fund was. We invited Tawnya and assistant wrangler Julie Tate to come to Atlanta and speak to our foundation staff and representatives from all the businesses about what they'd learned. Key takeaways included the importance of tapping into associates' own passions and areas of expertise. For example, many of the Mountain Sky associates were pre-med students, so community health initiatives were a natural fit for their giving. They also spoke about using all the assets they had at the ranch, not just the money in the fund, to have an impact. This included partnering with youth programs to connect kids with our horses, offering nonprofits the use of our "base camp" adventure facility and our challenge course, and hosting local seniors for a night of music and dancing. Every business has non-monetary assets—meeting spaces, expertise, brand power, facilities, local celebrities—that can be used for impact as well as for profit.

Today, each of our businesses has a thriving associate-led giving program. More than two hundred associates participate in volunteer committees, which have been collectively accountable for around $15 million to date. They also use their facilities, their expertise, and their brands in creative ways to amplify their impact.

Early on, we realized that the initiative could not be a free-for-all, driven entirely by the associates' personal interests. So we worked with them to set strategic priorities for funding—

causes that are close to their hearts *and* connected to their businesses. Each business has a guiding theme for their giving—an
overarching goal that aligns the associates as they decide how
to execute and manage their programs. It's not just a matter of
taking a pie and dividing it up between their favorite causes.
They have a North Star, a grand challenge, such as "reducing
childhood obesity in Georgia" or "improving the lives of veterans in our state." These can't just be solved with money; they
also require thinking strategically, building relationships, creating partnerships, measuring impact, and setting up systems
to sustain the progress that's made.

Scaling Impact Through Listening and Responding

Once we commit to an area, we don't want to just have a temporary impact. So we need to have the staying power and the
financial resources to stick with it. We want to generate momentum for the future, enroll partners who will be in it for the
long haul, and empower the recipients to keep that momentum
going. To do that, we need to dig deeper to understand the problems we're addressing and the various forces that have created
them.

In this regard, my own understanding has deepened enormously thanks to my oldest daughter, Dena, who works with
her mother, Diana, on her foundation, the Kendeda Fund
(named for Kenny, Dena, and Danielle, our three children).
Before joining the fund, Dena worked for several nonprofits,
including Outward Bound, Girls Inc., and Teach for America. She wanted to really understand what it was like on the
ground—raising money, running an organization, paying

staff, and operating programs. Now that she's in the position to help fund such organizations, she is able to do so with all that knowledge and understanding to inform her, and she's shared that invaluable experience with me as well. She's helped me to appreciate the nuts and bolts of making an impact and to play a more effective role as a partner and funder, and I hope I've passed that on to our associates. I'm also proud of how my eldest son, Kenny, has combined his personal passion and strategic business sense to grow the Atlanta Jewish Film Festival to become the largest such event in the world.

As someone who has successfully scaled for-profit businesses, it has often frustrated me to see philanthropic initiatives struggle to replicate and scale effective practices. To help me and our foundation understand and better address this challenge, in 2005 we invited Gary Walker, then the president of the research organization Public/Private Ventures, to address the foundation board. Gary was able to share real-life examples of how funders balanced the tension between wanting to take effective practices to scale and wanting to invest in innovative experiments that break new ground. It became clearer to me that we wanted to do both those things, so to some extent our philanthropy would always be a balancing act. The most important lesson from that day, however, was one that seems obvious in a business context but is easy to forget in a philanthropic one: know your customers.

What Gary pointed out was that foundations often make the mistake of thinking that their "customers" are the nonprofits to which they give grants. In fact, he explained, a foundation's customers are the individuals served by those grantee nonprofits. To truly be effective, our foundation needed to track the impact on those customers and continually adjust to ensure that our investments were aligned with their interests. Not only did this make perfect sense, it spoke directly to our core values. Out of that conversation, we made customer focus the explicit bedrock of our philanthropic approach.

A great example of the difference this makes came in 2013, when the Atlanta Falcons Youth Foundation got involved in efforts to improve the availability of fresh food in under-served areas of the city. Commonly labeled "food deserts," these neighborhoods had been the focus of a great deal of concern, including a state-funded task force in 2011, but change efforts had produced limited results. Our associates decided to go straight to the customer—the people living in those neighborhoods—and find out what they needed. One message they got right away: "Don't call us a food desert!" As John Bare, our family foundation SVP of programs, explains, vocabulary matters. "The food desert diagnosis too easily turns into a club used to beat families most in need. Being labeled a food desert makes a neighborhood undesirable, rather than a target of opportunity."

Being nagged by public health officials to eat more veggies wasn't effective, but that didn't mean people weren't interested in having access to fresh, high-quality produce. In talking to residents on the ground, one thing that became clear to our team was that the presence or absence of a grocery store—a key metric used to define a "food desert"—wasn't the biggest problem. Instead, people talked about things like not knowing how to cook and prepare fresh produce, not feeling welcome in certain stores, and wanting opportunities to grow their own food. Transportation and price were also challenges. Out of these conversations, the Georgia Food Oasis campaign was born in 2016. Working with people in the neighborhoods, it focused on offering cooking classes, reviving culinary traditions, and planting community gardens. Rather than trying to bring in large supermarkets, the campaign launched innovative retail solutions like small-scale neighborhood stores and pop-up markets at transit hubs. By 2016, our partners across the state were serving thirty-five million school meals featuring locally grown produce and had attracted twenty thousand new first-time shoppers to farmers' markets.

If you want to have an impact, it's imperative to close the gap between the well-meaning strategists and the people their strategies intend to serve. It doesn't matter if you're a for-profit or a nonprofit: putting people first and listening to what they want and need is the key to success.

Philanthropy from the Front Line

Between our various businesses, we support a wide range of causes and programs, with numerous partner organizations. Our PGA TOUR Superstore associates have partnered with the First Tee, an organization that teaches values to young people while getting them outside on the golf course. These programs, some of which are hosted in our stores, reach half a million children across the country. PGA TOUR Superstore also has store-based community funds that can focus on smaller local causes. The Mountain Sky fund continues to focus on families, children, and conservation, connecting young people to the beauty of the natural environment. Because our ranches are located in the heart of the Greater Yellowstone Ecosystem, we also saw an opportunity to be a leader in conservation, restoring native trout species to our creeks and improving wildlife habitats on our land while still maintaining a cattle operation. My daughter Danielle is deeply knowledgeable about conservation work and has played a critical role in these efforts. Recently, learning that our local Montana town, Livingston, has one of the highest suicide rates in the nation has spurred the team there to get involved in suicide-prevention and wellness initiatives. With the 2017 acquisition of West Creek Ranch, we also have a retreat venue dedicated to supporting nonprofits and providing them with an inspirational venue to come together to address issues of national significance, incubate ideas, and turn them into action.

The associates on every committee have come up with proposals that I don't believe our foundation team would have thought of alone. Everyone who serves on the Atlanta United Foundation committee is passionate about soccer, and many of them were once kids who wanted nothing more than a place to kick a ball with their friends. They understand how hard it can be for kids in urban communities to find safe, accessible, inclusive environments where they can play the game. They also know the incredible power of sports to keep kids healthy and active, connect them with others, break down barriers, and provide a path to educational and professional opportunity. Many of them have walked that path themselves. So when tasked with the mission of making their sport more accessible and inclusive in Georgia, they focused on the real barriers that kids in underprivileged communities face: transportation, safety, and cost. This led them to an innovative partnership with the city, the transit authority, and a local organization called Soccer in the Streets to launch StationSoccer, creating soccer pitches in unused space within MARTA transit stations

With my dear friend President Carter and my twins, Kylie and Max, prior to a Falcons game, 2004

BARACK OBAMA

Art —

I was watching the Falcons/Green Bay game, and was prompted to write a quick note to congratulate you not only on the new stadium and the team's recent success, but also on your insistence that food at the stadium was affordable to families. I was always grateful for your support when I ran for the presidency, but more importantly, I was always impressed by your commitment to your city and your people.

So good luck on the season, and I hope our paths cross again in the future.

Note I received from President Obama about our revolutionary food and beverage pricing approach at Mercedes-Benz Stadium, 2018

The napkin that sealed the deal for my purchase of the Atlanta Falcons, December 4, 2001

12/4/2001

FOR ATLANTA AND THE FALCONS 545,000,000.00 TO THE HERITAGE AND THE TRADITION IN THE PAST AND THE FUTURE —

Outside of one of our very first Home Depot stores, 1979 (*Pictured left to right:* Dennis Ross, Arthur Blank, Bernie Marcus, Pat Farrah, Ron Brill)

Serving pie with my daughter Kylie at the Mountain Sky Guest Ranch dinner ride, 2017

One of my treasured hobbies, horseback riding at Mountain Sky Guest Ranch, 2018

Celebrating Atlanta United's MLS Championship win after the parade through Atlanta, 2018

Atlanta United games are a special experience at Mercedes-Benz Stadium, 2018

One of my favorite activities, interacting with our Atlanta United fans, 2017

Mercedes-Benz Stadium, a beautiful structure that represents so much more than just the building, 2018

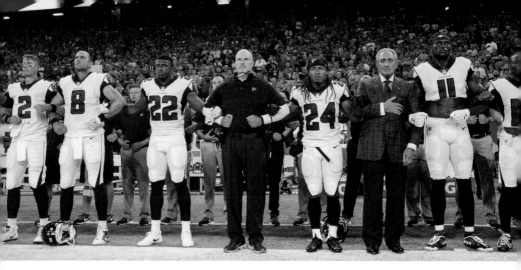

Linking arms for social justice in solidarity with Falcons players and coaching staff, September 24, 2017

Sharing a fun moment with Falcons quarterback Matt Ryan prior to a game, 2019

Michael Vick honored with other Falcons legends (pictured with wide receiver Roddy White) at the final regular season game at the Georgia Dome, 2017

The Strong Heart Warrior, as depicted in Dave McGary's *Point of No Return*, a physical representation of the core value "Lead by Example" in our offices

One of my favorite photos of my father, Max, and brother, Michael, outside of our family business, Oes Pharmacy, in 1940

The foundation of my values began with my family, pictured here with my mother, Molly Blank, and my brother, Michael Blank, 2013

The First Tee is an
organization very near
and dear to my heart,
and I love that our golf
business continues to
support it, 2019

The Westside Flag
Football League is one of
the great successes of our
Westside efforts, with
over 650 neighborhood
kids involved in the
program, 2018

Atlanta's Westside, once home to Dr. King, has a wealth of history but is one of the most
disadvantaged neighborhoods in our country. In building Mercedes-Benz Stadium just
a stone's throw away, we committed to the long-term revitalization of this community,
2019.

where kids from different neighborhoods can come together to play the "beautiful game."

Supporting the military has always been a priority across our business, but a few years ago, we decided to formalize this commitment as part of an associate-led giving program, and so the Overwatch Fund was born. The fund is managed by associates from across our businesses who have a personal connection to the military, including many veterans and those with family members in active service. Their grantmaking has focused on helping veterans fulfill basic needs like food and housing, supporting their well-being and mental health, and facilitating successful transitions back to civilian life.

Because of their personal connection to service, our committee members really understand the challenges facing veterans. A few years ago, they were evaluating a possible grant to the Shepherd Center's SHARE Military Initiative for veterans with traumatic brain injuries (TBIs). When talking to the staff, they noticed something important. The program's eligibility criteria ruled out participants who were using drugs. Our committee members knew how many veterans struggled with substance misuse, and it bothered them that this valuable program would be unavailable to so many who needed its help. But rather than walk away, they came back with a new proposal—a program through which veterans who need support with substance misuse can now also have access to the care they need for TBIs.

It takes people who are involved at the ground level to truly understand the needs of a particular community or interest group, and know how to use the funding most effectively. They also know how to leverage their particular assets and their brand in ways the foundation never could. And through all this, we're nurturing a commitment to giving back in all our associates that will continue whether they work for us or move on to other endeavors. Many have gone on to volunteer outside of their work with us and to donate their own money to causes they care about.

I would love to see more companies adopting an associate-led approach to their social impact and philanthropic work. There are few things in life that feel better than giving, and everyone benefits from the positive energy that is generated when people are directly empowered to make a difference. With so much money concentrated among corporations and wealthy individuals, it's easy to think that philanthropy is yet another privilege of the elites. But it doesn't have to be that way. As the corporate world takes strides in recognizing its responsibility to give back, companies also have an opportunity to share the power of giving with their own associates. In so doing, they redistribute not just wealth but the extraordinary benefits that come from being able to help others and give back. They will contribute to that precious sense of meaning and purpose that we all seek and foster a lifelong commitment to giving among the people who work for them.

Our neighborhoods, our communities, our country, and our planet face so many challenges, and sometimes it can seem as though new ones appear every day. As I write these words, the entire world is reeling from the personal and economic impact of the COVID-19 pandemic, and like many companies, we are scrambling to adapt and to do everything we can to help. We're continuing to pay and provide benefits to our staff, including our hourly-wage associates, and we're funding relief efforts in Georgia and Montana. One of the things that has most touched me personally is how many of our associates wanted to volunteer to help. They've learned that one of the most powerful antidotes to stress and anxiety is the act of giving. With the mandate for social distancing, there have been limited opportunities for hands-on involvement, but it's evident that the value of service has deeply taken root in our family of businesses, and that makes me very proud. It also makes me hopeful about our future. In times like these, people from all walks of life come together in remarkable ways, and I truly believe that we will rise to this challenge and to whatever new challenges present themselves in the years to come.

We need people working at every level of scale, from small local charities to global initiatives. We need to harness the wealth of the most privileged and the power of business and government, but we also need to tap into the passion and creativity of individuals everywhere. If giving back can become part of what people do every day when they go to work, we can truly make progress, despite the enormity of the challenges we face. And in the process, we all get the extraordinary gift of connection. Companies connect to communities. Associates connect to neighbors. Corporate leaders connect to civic leaders. Organizations connect to others with similar missions. And people connect to people, united in a common cause. Collectively, we can do so much more than we ever could apart.

Chapter 8

||||||||||||||||||

We Want the Wheels to Wobble (a Little)

Humanity can thrive only when challenged, when called
upon to answer new demands, to reach out for new heights.

—RABBI ABRAHAM JOSHUA HESCHEL

"You should start a soccer team!"

The suggestion didn't come from a trusted business advisor or a market strategist. No, it came from someone whose opinion mattered much more to me: my then tween son Josh. It was about 2010, and we were just getting serious about the monumental undertaking of building the new stadium. I'd also recently acquired the struggling PGA TOUR Superstore retail chain and was tasked with turning it around. The last thing I needed was a new venture. And yet—

"C'mon, Dad. It would be so cool. Atlanta should have an MLS team!"

Throughout the early 2000s, while I'd been learning the ropes of the NFL, Josh had seemed to practically live in his soccer kit (although his mom drew the line at cleats on our floors). An avid fan and a talented player, he started playing in grade school and worked his way up to the elite youth leagues. He was so dedicated to the sport that he'd come home every day after practice, ask me to move the cars out of the garage, and spend hours kicking a soccer ball against the wall.

At first, the game that Josh loved so much was a foreign world to me. When I was a kid, you played baseball, football, or basketball, and I chose the first two of those three, as well as running track. In the seventies and eighties, when my three elder children were growing up, soccer was slowly becoming more common in America's streets, parks, and even schools, but none of them had much interest in the game. My oldest son, Kenny, had a chance to play in grade school, but he was less than enthusiastic. In fact, he once decided to lay down in the middle of the pitch to take a nap! It was not until the nineties that soccer truly took center stage in the country at large, and a few years later, in my family. America played host to the men's World Cup tournament in 1994, and in 1996, just a year before Josh was born, Major League Soccer kicked off its first games. In 1999, the US women's national team captured the hearts of a generation as they triumphantly won the World Cup on home turf. By 2010, when Josh made his business proposal to me, more American kids were enrolled in soccer than in any sport other than basketball.[1]

I could have doubled down on what I knew and told him, "No, son, I'm in the football business." But I'm in the sports and entertainment business, and for a younger American audience, for a Hispanic American audience, and for the huge immigrant population in our growing city, soccer is the sport of choice. In Atlanta alone, there were tens of thousands of kids playing. I'm also involved in initiatives to combat childhood obesity and recognized the many positive health benefits for boys and girls of a sport that has them running up and down a field in the fresh air for hours. This was a great chance to prac-

tice inverted management—to listen and respond to those closest to demographics our other businesses struggled to reach.
Besides, I had grown to truly love the game. By this point, I'd
spent years on the sidelines watching Josh excel in Atlanta's
youth leagues. In my role as his unofficial team photographer,
I'd been struck, again and again, by the diversity of the sport
and its potential to unify. My camera captured the same ex-
pressions of joy, determination, celebration, and despair on
young faces of every color. Soccer truly is the world's sport and
the sport of America's future generations. It represents how
our nation is changing—and for the better. That's the kind of
change I want to be part of.

The notion of a soccer team in Atlanta had been floated before in conversations with MLS commissioner Don Garber,
but the timing had never been right. The league had been worried about whether this international sport would find enough
of a fan base in Atlanta. Plus, there was nowhere for a soccer team to play, and we were hesitant to invest in building a
soccer-specific facility. I'd always had a gut feeling, however,
that Atlanta would embrace soccer. The city has a huge and
fast-growing immigrant population, as well as a large millen-
nial demographic. In 2010, with the ink not yet dried on our
earliest sketches for the new stadium, the opportunity seemed
compelling. I had a lot on my plate; we all did. But if we did it
now, we could build soccer into the stadium from the ground
up. The entrepreneur in me got excited about launching a
brand-new venture—one that didn't have anyone else's fingerprints on it—and being part of a sport with so much growth
potential. And yes, the father in me saw a golden opportunity
to make my son happy.

Soon, I'd have another very personal reason to love soccer.

On the sidelines in 2012, I met Angie Macuga, the mother of one of Josh's teammates, Drew. Angie and I bonded as we watched our sons racing up and down the field, and I came to deeply respect her dedication to her children. She was the epitome of a soccer mom, in the very best sense of the term, driving tens of thousands of miles a year to cheer on her kids. She knew the game far better than me, and frequently I turned to her for technical explanations of events on the pitch. I'll always be grateful for the role soccer played in bringing Angie, Drew, Emily, and Morgan into my life.

A Values-Driven Startup

From the moment we officially announced the then unnamed soccer team, on April 16, 2014, it had a life of its own. I'd intuited that Atlanta would embrace the sport, but I could not possibly have anticipated the energy, passion, and commitment that our fans showed from day one. We'd picked a downtown rooftop venue for the invitation-only announcement, worried that we didn't yet have enough of a fan base to support a large public event. This was football country, after all, and we were anticipating that it would take time to get Atlantans excited about soccer. At the last minute, we decided it might be a good idea to set up a kind of festival across the street where the announcement could be streamed and fans could gather. We'd just launched our website and social media channels, so we thought a few dozen might show up. I was scheduled to make a surprise landing by helicopter with Commissioner Garber, and as we flew in over the venue, I could hardly believe what I saw. A couple of thousand people were gathered in the street.

As I stepped up to make my remarks, I realized the crowd was chanting "Un-cle Ar-thur! Un-cle Ar-thur!" I had no idea why they'd decided to give me this title, but I couldn't have been prouder to be an honorary uncle to this team and its fans. I also couldn't have been prouder to be a father, as I looked at Josh, sitting in the front row. A few weeks later we broke ground on the new stadium, and I announced that the very first event to be played after our planned opening in the spring of 2017 would be the MLS team's inaugural home game.

There was something special about our fans from the start. We took a grassroots approach, focusing on our avid supporters and encouraging them to create a club mentality and a sense of community long before there was even a team. Drew was among our most dedicated community builders, showing up at countless fan events and promoting our brand. I loved attending those promotional events myself—drinking a beer in an Irish pub with supporters and chatting with them about what they wanted the new team to be. It was a markedly different culture from the NFL, where owners are traditionally more removed from the fans. The informal soccer-club attitude gave me an opportunity to get direct feedback, and this was invaluable as we envisioned the franchise.

Building Atlanta United was the most entrepreneurial venture I've been involved with since we launched The Home Depot. My other businesses were each already established, so while we brought our own creativity to bear in turning them around, expanding them, and making them successful, in each case we were starting with an existing brand, culture, and business model. Atlanta United was envisioned and created from the ground up, and as such, it's my favorite example of how our core values apply in a startup situation.

We put people first, quite literally. Three years before there was a team, a name, a stadium, or anything else, I set out to hire a president and CEO for the club. A lot of people avoid hiring for leadership roles so far in advance because they say the cost is too high. But that's not how I see it. It's a critical part of the startup costs, and it should be budgeted for as early as possible. Getting the right leader in place is perhaps the most important investment one can make in the formation of a company. At The Home Depot, we thought of this as part of what we called pre-opening expenses for every new store. Those costs can't be avoided, but because they allow you to get the store up and running with an army of trained associates who understand your culture, they are worth every penny. Unlike many MLS teams, who hired their executives primarily from within the league, I decided to conduct a worldwide search. Soccer is an international sport, and I reasoned that if we wanted the very best, there was a good chance we'd find that person outside the US. Hiring Darren Eales from the UK's Tottenham Hotspurs to lead Atlanta United was the best decision we could have made, and hiring him early made all the difference because he was a world-class executive who could help us shape every aspect of the new club.

Another key advantage to hiring Darren early was that he was able to attract others of a similar caliber to join him. This included two-time US World Cup team captain Carlos Bocanegra as our technical director and Argentine soccer legend Gerardo "Tata" Martino as our first coach. Together, they were able to attract young, dynamic players like Miguel Almirón and Josef Martinez, convincing them there was a bright future in MLS rather than the European leagues. Time and time again, I put my trust in Darren's instincts, particularly when it came to these key hires. Bocanegra had no front office experience. And as for Tata, he spoke only Spanish. When Darren told me he was planning to hire a guy who didn't speak a word of English, I thought he was joking.

"How's he going to coach the non-Spanish-speaking players?" I asked.

Darren didn't miss a beat. "*Fútbol* is its own language," he told me confidently. And he was right. Tata worked magic with the team, and his warm personality more than made up for any language gaps. He instantly made everyone feel understood. I always used to joke that even though he and I could barely hold a conversation, we loved each other just the same.

Coming from a storied Premier League club steeped in tradition, but with a love for America that dated back to his collegiate days as an All-American at Brown University, Darren was excited about the entrepreneurial challenge of Atlanta's new club. The fact that his first visit coincided with Thanksgiving helped to seal the deal—he got turkey dinner several days in a row! Darren also shared my passion for youth soccer and was committed to helping us develop a youth academy in the tradition of the European soccer leagues from the outset. Our vision was to nurture homegrown talent for the team and also promote the sport in our state and our country. He spent the time leading up to the 2017 launch researching and connecting with the Atlanta soccer fan base, checking out training grounds options, hiring technical and business operations staff, and scouting players.

We asked our fans about everything and involved them in all the key decisions. A case in point was the choice of name and uniform. I wanted to ensure that our fans had a voice in the branding of the team. Darren felt the same way. "We don't want to impose an artificial narrative on our fans," he said. "This is their club, and the name needs to be their name." The supporters group had run a poll, but it came back with no clear winner. When we reached out to our broader founding members list, we asked them to rate words and phrases that they identified with the club and the city. A clear message began to emerge. The fans wanted a traditional name, like those in the European leagues. They didn't want a catchy American-style club name, like the Chicago Fire or the San Jose Earthquakes. The highest rated terms were Atlanta, United, and FC (for Football Club). I loved the fact that the message from our diverse fan base was unity. It spoke to everything I hoped our club would represent.

We had our name: *Atlanta United*. Or, we almost had it. A hurdle arose when we went to the league for approval. There was already an MLS club called United (in Washington DC), and the proposal to add another was politically sensitive. The name is extremely common in the English professional leagues, with fourteen of the ninety-two teams carrying the moniker, but some people resisted the notion. I didn't want to be the owner who threw his weight around in the league, so I tried to be diplomatic. But inwardly I was determined not to back down. Why? Because our fans had spoken clearly, and it was our job to respond. It was the right brand for our club and our city. Eventually, we prevailed, with the compromise of adding "FC" to the name as a further point of distinction. Don Garber graciously told me later that he's glad he acquiesced. United was simply the right name for our team.

The announcement of the team name and unveiling of our logo was a key opportunity to engage our fans. By this point we had twenty-one thousand founding members, all of whom had paid deposits on season tickets, and we invited every one of them. When *Sports Illustrated* leaked the name a couple of weeks before the event, we were worried that no one would think it worth showing up. We couldn't have been more wrong. I was in the middle of doing media interviews with Darren in a bus outside the venue when we got the message that the event was being delayed for an hour because the line was so long. More than 4,500 fans packed the venue, chanting and wearing our team colors of red, black, and gold. Those who couldn't fit inside climbed up on the walls and the gate.

We truly didn't assume we understood what soccer fans needed and all the ways in which they were different than our NFL fans. The same turned out to be true of soccer players. This point was driven home to me when we proudly showed Darren the designs for the soccer team locker rooms, which were to be identical to the Falcons' locker rooms, including a large plunge pool. There was nothing second-class about these digs. But when Darren saw them, he laughed.

"You've done a great job, Arthur," he said, "but you know what? We don't have a squad of fifty-four, and our players aren't the size of giants!" He proposed that we could reduce the size of the pool to fit eight regular-sized people, and with all the costs we saved, we built a mezzanine dining room, which is what the players use during the pre-match and where they can bring their families post-match.

Perhaps nowhere was the football-*fútbol* divide clearer than when it came to beer. Football fans drink traditional brands like Bud Light, Heineken, or Coors. Soccer fans prefer to start with craft beers and microbrews. So we set up the concession stands in such a way that we could pour each fanbase its beverage of choice throughout a game.

We also gave Atlanta United supporters room to create their own twists on MLS rituals and match-day traditions, bringing players closer to the fans and creating a sense of intimacy that is unusual in North American professional sports and unheard of in European soccer.

I was sensitive to ensuring that our soccer team and fans never felt as though they were playing second fiddle to the Falcons. That very first day, I'd promised the fans, "There will never be an MLS game in Atlanta where NFL lines are shown on the pitch." So the stadium was designed from the beginning with soccer in mind. The pitch was laid out to FIFA standards, meaning that future World Cup games could be played there, and we added soccer warm-up and locker rooms, and a special entrance to the field for the soccer team. The field-level seating was retractable, making it feel like an authentic soccer pitch.

There were countless opportunities for innovation in the Atlanta United journey. One area in which we quickly decided to diverge from the league's common practices was in our approach to signing players. MLS teams tended to make a name for themselves by signing an aging star from Europe with huge brand recognition. Think David Beckham and the LA Galaxy or Thierry Henry and the New York Red Bulls. Darren and I had other plans. Knowing we wanted to put a competitive team on the pitch while also being economically savvy, we used our capital to sign young, talented players straight out of Latin America who were emerging stars, not fading ones. We gave guys who needed it most a chance to play, and they have not let us down. We created a coaching environment in which they could develop into their full potential. We added some veteran players who could lead the locker room, play some defense, and provide instant credibility. But we also turned the young strikers loose to try to outscore other teams. It worked—and by 2018, other MLS teams were jetting to South America looking for "stars like Atlanta United has." We also demonstrated our commitment to supporting homegrown talent from the very beginning, establishing the Soccer Academy for promising youth players.

Project Lemonade

"It's not going to be ready."

I'd heard those words many times as 2015 drew to a close, but usually they came phrased as a question, a possibility, or a worst-case scenario. Now, they were simply a statement of fact. The stadium was overbudget and behind schedule, and there was no chance that Atlanta United would be able to start their season on the new field in the spring of 2017 as planned.

This was a blow, for many reasons. Thirty thousand soccer fans had bought season tickets, proud that they would be the first through the gates of the new stadium. It had seemed fitting to me that Atlanta United would be the first team to take to the field, reinforcing the message that they were anything but an afterthought. However, it was not to be.

So, we scrambled to adapt. Because that's what you do with a startup. Anyone who's founded a company will tell you that setbacks are the rule, not the exception. The team would need to play their first nine matches at a temporary venue: Georgia Tech's Bobby Dodd Stadium. It was a far cry from the start we'd hoped our team would have, playing in a state-of-the-art venue built specifically for them. Bobby Dodd is a storied, century-old college football stadium with a narrow field and hard steel bleachers. It was a college venue, so it wasn't set up to serve beer, and it took a great deal of persuasion, including a significant share of the revenue, to get Georgia Tech to agree to do so. That was okay, though. The beer wasn't about making money for us; it was about giving the fans the experience they expected.

One of the tasks I dreaded was telling Darren. He'd been working so hard to engage our fan base, and he'd feel terrible that we would not be able to give them the season start we'd promised. I was at the aircraft hangar that day and asked him to come and meet me there. He took the news surprisingly well. Later, he confessed that he'd interpreted the unusual meeting venue as a sign he was about to be fired, so the actual bad news seemed mild by comparison!

How would we take this negative and make it into a positive? We called it Project Lemonade. And it wasn't just spin—what we realized was that this was an opportunity to do something every startup must do: beta testing. We could try things out in an environment where we could easily make changes and adapt. Bobby Dodd, for all its limitations, was a great laboratory for our fledgling club and its fans. We could see what worked and what didn't, and we could take the things that worked with us to the new stadium.

Our first game was a sellout success. We were shocked. Season ticket sales had well exceeded our expectations, but we still never imagined we'd fill the stadium. More than fifty-five thousand fans waited in traffic and stood in line to get into that old stadium. Don Garber, the MLS commissioner, couldn't believe that these people had all paid for tickets. In fact, if we'd had more seats, we could have sold those too. Later, he told me he never thought he'd see anything like that in our league. My driver had to navigate through a throng of marching, singing, banner-waving supporters. People crowded into the narrow bleachers and stood in more hopelessly long lines to get beer (unused to serving alcohol, the stadium staff were overwhelmed and unprepared). They cheered, chanted, and sang. I never thought I'd find myself humbled and inspired by soccer fans, but that's exactly how I felt at that first match. We lost, 2–1, but it didn't matter. We'd won the city's heart.

At Bobby Dodd, we tried out special team rituals, like our Golden Spike, inspired by Atlanta's history as a railroad terminus. One of the greatest traditions to come out of that era was the fact that our fans, caught up in the excitement, got out of their seats at the beginning of the match and never sat back down. In part, this was an unintended consequence of the cramped, hot, uncomfortable steel bleachers, but from that day on, our fans stood in the pouring rain or the blazing sun. And to this day, even though Mercedes-Benz Stadium is fitted from top to bottom with those comfortable, twenty-one-inch seats, the soccer fans stand. It creates a truly electric atmosphere.

It was during one of those games at Bobby Dodd that we realized a key piece was missing from our designs for the new stadium. In soccer, there are groups of dedicated, organized fans known as Supporter Groups, who always sit in a specific section behind the goal at one end of the field. They get the crowd fired up, waving huge banners and chanting. The supporters have a leader, known as the capo, who stands on a podium, the capo stand, down at the field level and leads the chants. It's the focal point of the fan experience, and the source of the energy that the fans transmit to our team. We also used the capo stand for the anthem, for the Golden Spike ritual, and for honoring the Man of the Match. But in designing Mercedes-Benz Stadium, we'd completely overlooked this critical feature. Indeed, we'd planned two of our premium field-level suites for that area of the stadium.

When Darren pointed this out, I wasn't happy. Those suites were an important revenue source, and they'd already been sold. But our number one job was to honor the fans, and there was no question that the fans would feel cheated if they looked down to where their capo should be standing holding a megaphone and instead saw a bunch of VIP guests. So we moved the VIPs to other suites, refunding the difference in cost, and went to work figuring out how the premium suites could be repurposed as a capo stand on soccer match days.

Construction was continuing at a fever pitch. Not being ready for the start of the Atlanta United season had been an inconvenience, but not being ready for the NFL opener would be a disaster. The league would have done its best to accommodate us, and we could have scheduled all our preseason games on the road, but so much was riding on the stadium being ready, from fan expectations to sponsorship dollars. Steve Cannon, who had come over from Mercedes-Benz USA to be our new CEO in the midst of all this, felt like the main thing he did that summer was deliver bad news. Budget increases. Steel shortages. Mechanical problems. Delays. We poured every resource we had available into that building. In the final three months, we had thousands of people working around the clock, three shifts a day. It was like a carefully choreographed dance. Teams worked around one another; engineers tested, remediated, and reinforced the building; the art collection was hung; the four thousand miles of fiber-optic cable were connected;

the vast LED screens were installed. I was beginning to understand why Falcons president Rich McKay, who'd done this before in Tampa, had told me bluntly: "Stadiums take years off your life." To this day, he won't let me forget that when I hired him, I'd promised he wouldn't have to build another one for a long time—and yet, just a few years later, we were doing exactly that.

The greatest challenge was the retractable petaled roof—the signature of the stadium's design. It worked, but not fast enough. If we were to open it during an event, we needed to know we could close it at the touch of a button should Atlanta's famously changeable weather require it. I vividly recall the day when Rich, Steve, and Bill Darden showed up to meet with me looking like someone had just died. Before a word had been said, I knew they'd come to tell me the roof wasn't going to be functional for the early-season games. And they were clearly not expecting me to take the news well. Fair enough—I'm often the one pushing back against limitations and challenging the team to do the seemingly impossible. But in this case, I knew they weren't making excuses, and there's no sense in applying pressure to a situation that's already pushed to the limit. This wasn't an outcome that could be changed by trying harder. So as they explained the situation at hand, I put aside my disappointment.

"We're not building this stadium for the next three months," I said. "We're building it for the next thirty years. Let's not act like this is a defeat. What people will remember most is how they were treated here. So let's focus on training our associates and giving fans a great time. And when the roof is ready to work, it will work."

Rich, Steve, and Bill looked surprised—and relieved. In July, we announced that the roof would stay closed for the beginning of the season. But the stadium would be open, whatever it took. And it was. The Falcons took to the field for a preseason game in front of a full house of fans on August 26, 2017.

When the time came for Atlanta United to make its debut on the new pitch, however, our fans and associates were asking a question I never expected to hear. Would it be as good as Bobby Dodd? That old stadium had created such an atmosphere of community and excitement, and they were concerned it might get lost in the newer, bigger venue. Those worries, however, turned out to be unfounded. In its first year of existence, Atlanta United shattered a twenty-two-year-old league attendance record and changed team-building in America forever. And the following year, in only its second season, the team won the MLS championship. ESPN called our launch "the most successful of a new team in the history of North American professional sports."[2] And as exciting as it is to watch the team on the pitch, I find myself spending half of every game watching the people in the stands. What happens there during every match is as meaningful to me as any trophy. We've inspired a passion in the fans that is unmatched in American soccer. When I look around at the diversity of our fan base, the joy on their faces, the goodwill, and the sense of connectedness, I have a new appreciation for why they call it the "beautiful game."

Bottom line, we've been successful with Atlanta United because we've followed not "the rules" but rather *our rules*. We've stuck to our values and listened to our fans. We've never compromised on quality. We've honored our sport's global traditions, but we've never been afraid to try new things.

Innovate Continuously

What keeps a company great (and a person, for that matter) is nonstop reinvention. Whether you're launching a brand-new venture or leading a long-established brand, you need to constantly ask, "What can we do better? What can we do differently?" If you're always in motion, no one can catch you. That's why one of our core values is "innovate continuously."

When you hear the term *innovation,* your mind probably conjures up technological marvels like self-driving cars or 3-D printers. But while those certainly deserve the name, innovation also has a less flashy meaning. It's about creating something new, but it's also about effecting change in something established. This second meaning is where many organizations fall short. It's one thing to be innovative when you're starting with a blank slate, dreaming up a new company or a product. It's another to continually innovate when you've been doing something for years, especially if it's successful. Too many companies settle into complacency once they've found a formula that works and keeps shareholders happy. They don't want to risk throwing things off balance by trying something new.

The Home Depot was a massive innovation when we launched. Our stores were far bigger than our competitors'. Our business model was different: we purchased directly from manufacturers, cutting out the middleman, and we kept our prices low, relying on high sales volume, driven by great service, which led to customer loyalty. We were proud of these innovations, and the market loved them. But that didn't stop us from continuing to innovate, in little ways, every day.

Just because you've done something one way for a decade doesn't mean that's the way you should keep doing it. Innovation means constantly seeking new ways to improve results and move above and beyond what seems possible. That's why we say innovate *continuously*. It's not about having light bulb moments of novelty; it's about the everyday commitment to stay one step ahead of the market and the competition. Among my collection of classic motivational posters is one depicting a lion chasing a gazelle. The message is simple: every morning that gazelle wakes up and knows it must run faster than the fastest lion, or be killed. And every morning that lion wakes up and knows it must outrun the slowest gazelle or it will starve. It doesn't matter if you're a lion or a gazelle; when the sun comes up, you'd better be running.

Innovation can mean many things. It might mean improvements in quality. It might mean new products or services. It might mean new processes that make the company's operations more efficient. From my perspective, everything in a company is open for reinvention, except the company's core values. These stay steady, and the best innovations find new ways to honor and uphold them.

Humans are extraordinarily creative creatures, but we're also creatures of habit. We naturally fall into comfortable patterns, especially when they've proven to be successful. To continually innovate means you have to keep pushing. You can't ever sit back and just run on autopilot. I always tell our associates: If the car is just driving safely and smoothly down the road, you're not innovating. We want the wheels to wobble—a little. Of course, we don't want the wheels to fall off, but unless you feel as though they might, you're probably taking things too slowly and too safely.

To instill a culture of continuous innovation in a company, leaders need to ensure that the road is cleared of unnecessary speed bumps and overly stringent traffic rules. Too much bureaucracy will kill innovation before it has even begun, and an overly centralized, top-down management structure will always constrain people's entrepreneurial spirit. You need to give associates an appropriate amount of freedom to try new things, make mistakes, and even fail without fear of overly negative repercussions. At PGA TOUR Superstore, one of the ways they encourage this is by running annual offsite training events that are only for hourly associates, not managers. They get to go to a nice resort in Florida and learn about the products they'll be selling, directly from the manufacturers. In too many companies, events like this are a perk for management. By skipping that level and giving the associates the direct experience, PGA TOUR Superstore encourages them to feel responsible for translating what they've learned back into their stores. They're not waiting for their managers to tell them how.

At The Home Depot, we used to call this the "invisible fence" style of management. Have you ever seen a dog that runs across the lawn until it hits an invisible fence that buzzes its collar and stops it in its tracks? It's a very effective training method, and one that I've been reminded of recently, having welcomed two new puppies into the family. Translated to management, the idea is that there are limits to people's autonomy and freedom to make decisions, but those limits are not always made explicit until they are crossed. This encourages people to strike out and take risks, rather than playing it safe. It incentivizes entrepreneurialism. We want people to embrace the attitude that it's better to ask for forgiveness than for permission. And when they occasionally do go too far and cross the invisible boundary, we use it as an opportunity to mentor, educate, and build trust rather than simply punish a mistake. The fence is in different places for different people, depending on how much trust they have earned. Dick Sullivan still uses this metaphor at PGA TOUR Superstore. He's built on it, as well. He likes to tell his team that there are three kinds of dogs: those that run up to the fence and stop, those that jump over the fence but come back, and those that jump over the fence and make you go out there and get them. "You don't want all of your people to be the first or third kind of dog," he says, "although for some jobs they might be just fine."

One of the most important outcomes of the invisible fence approach is that people gain confidence in themselves and their ability to make decisions, be creative, and take risks. And they get the message that their leaders have confidence in them and trust them. Confidence is a valuable quality in associates because it fuels innovation, but it can too easily be stamped out in an overly controlling and risk-averse management culture. I've seen this play out again and again in numerous business settings, and even on the football field. As a rule, I never get involved in the football side of the Falcons operation—I respect the expertise of our coaching staff and let them do their job. But I made an exception one time. It was the opening game of the season, against a very good team, and we were nearing the end of the fourth quarter, down three points. Our coach at the time, Mike Smith, elected to go for a field goal, which gave us the three points needed to tie the game and go into overtime, rather than go for the touchdown that could have won the game but also risked losing it. Oftentimes, that's a smart call—especially in a critical playoff game. But this was the start of the season, and I was aware that what the team needed right then, perhaps even more than a win, was the knowledge that their coach trusted them and had confidence in them.

We lost the game in overtime. The loss wasn't a big deal, but that insight about the team's confidence was critical to me, so much so that the following day, I broke my own rule and took the coach aside. "Look, Smitty," I said. "I wouldn't normally say something like this, but here's a lesson I've learned in business. Sometimes the message we send to our associates is more important than whether they succeed or fail in any given task. It's early in the season, and our players need to know we have confidence in them. I just want you to know that I'll always support you in sending that message, even if it means we lose the game because the risk doesn't pay off."

Business, like sports, is full of wins and losses. Sometimes, you're going to go for the win and fumble, or get knocked on your ass by a two-hundred-fifty-pound linebacker. But if you don't go for it, your business is guaranteed to stagnate. What keeps an organization living, and innovating, over the long run, is that people feel empowered and trusted to try.

Get Comfortable Being Uncomfortable

Clinging to a small handhold on the cliff face, I reminded myself, "Don't look down." I just needed to lift my right foot about six inches, to the next ledge, but it seemed to have become welded in its current position. As much as I willed my foot to move, the signals were not getting through. Fighting the urge to glance at the drop beneath me, I let my gaze follow the rope upward instead. A woman was moving steadily up the rock wall above me, looking as if she'd been doing this all her life.

Below me, I heard muttered curses and surmised that her husband was not finding the climb so easy. "Don't look down." Taking a deep breath, I wrenched my uncooperative foot away from the rock and planted it on the ledge. Then the other foot. Then my right hand reached for a new indentation in the rock. Then the other hand. "Keep breathing. Keep moving."

My companions on the cliff face that day, now several decades past, were President Jimmy Carter and his wife, Rosalynn. Although the Carters are dear friends and I relish any opportunity to spend time with them, I can't say that particular activity was my idea of fun, and I suspect the president would agree. But that wasn't why we were doing it. We were participating in a training led by Outward Bound, an organization that is very dear to my heart. In fact, I've often said that if I had to pick only one organization among the many that I support, it would be that one, because it has had more impact on my own life than any other organization I've been involved with. Founded in 1941 by Kurt Hahn and Lawrence Holt, Outward Bound uses wilderness adventures and activities to help people develop qualities Hahn believed to be essential to human thriving: "an enterprising curiosity, an undefeatable spirit, tenacity in pursuit, readiness for sensible self-denial, and above all, compassion." Outward Bound offers this invaluable lesson: *we are capable of more than we think we are.* Most of us tend to live inside a box made up of what we believe our constraints to be, and unless we're challenged or tested, we don't even realize it. It is deeply empowering to discover that we can find our own way out of difficult situations, overcome seemingly insurmountable challenges, and triumph over our fears and insecurities.

Put another way, Outward Bound has helped me—and

countless others—get more comfortable being uncomfortable. And there are few, if any, more important skills for success in business and in life. It's impossible to innovate if you're not able to withstand feelings like insecurity, instability, and anxiety. The innovator is balanced on that cliff face, hand outstretched, reaching for the new ledge without knowing for sure that it will hold. They are called on again and again to make smart decisions under pressure, to adapt on the fly, to come up with creative solutions, and not to give up in the face of fear and uncertainty.

If we shy away from uncomfortable feelings, we'll never get the opportunity to find out what we're really made of—on a cliff face or in the boardroom. When I speak to young people who want to pursue an entrepreneurial life, I always remind them that it will require courage. And the courage to remain in that uncomfortable zone—to feel the wheels wobbling and still drive with a steady hand—is something that grows with repeated practice. That's why I've taken numerous Outward Bound trainings, and I encouraged every manager at The Home Depot to do the same. It wasn't just a team-building gimmick or a form of entertainment. It was important training for living one of our core values. And our associates knew it. In fact, Bernie, who hated the outdoors unless it came in the form of a golf course, once confessed to me that he'd gone around trying to find people who didn't feel they had benefited from the trainings because he didn't understand why we kept doing them, and he couldn't find one person. Everyone acknowledged that they'd learned new things about themselves and discovered new capacities as a result of taking the trainings. Reluctantly, he agreed to let them continue, although he drew the line at participating himself.

An added benefit of the Outward Bound trainings is the way they level traditional hierarchies. It's healthy for associates to come together in unstructured relationships, peer to peer, and work together in unfamiliar circumstances where the usual rules don't apply. Dick Sullivan likes to tell the story of a training he attended back in the Home Depot days where he was the only vice president among the group. Everyone else was younger and held positions of far less responsibility. But as the instructor quizzed them on their knowledge of the outdoors, Dick quickly realized that in this situation, he was the least experienced person present. He'd never rock-climbed, purified his own water, read a topographical map, or even gone to the bathroom in the woods. "I may've been vice president, but I was at the bottom out here—no corner tent for me—and I needed these people to survive," he said.

My favorite Outward Bound story involved a guy named George Collins, from our Tampa offices. He was one of the best district managers we had at the time and would have been a natural candidate for promotion, but there was just one problem. George had a debilitating fear of heights that prevented him from being able to fly. One day, George was among a bunch of our associates who were participating in an Outward Bound training that involved a ropes course. I was walking down the road beneath the course when I happened to glance upward.

"Holy shit," I exclaimed. "George is up in the tree." Afterward, when he was safely back on the ground, he told me jubilantly, "I think I may have gotten over my fear of flying." Soon after, he was promoted to regional vice-president, a job that required him to fly all over the place.

Every one of us is guaranteed to find ourselves in stressful situations, in business and in life. When that happens, like it or not, we find out what we're made of. Once in a while, however, it's worth deliberately putting yourself in the discomfort zone—not for its own sake but because you care more about what's possible on the other side than you care about your temporary feelings. I learned this as a kid because I grew up with a source of ongoing discomfort: a stutter. I'm grateful to my mother that she always encouraged me to speak up anyway, and she taught me that it didn't matter if I had a little difficulty getting the words out. By the time I left for college, I'd embraced the discomfort. I'd sit in the front row in every class and raise my hand to answer the professor's questions. I knew the other kids were thinking, "Oh no, here we go again. A five-minute answer to a question that should take thirty seconds." But I kept doing it.

Years later, I was playing golf with Jack Welch, and I asked him, "How do you deal with your stutter?"

His reply? "My mother would constantly tell me, 'What you have to say is important.' "

That said everything. We all have limitations, whether they be physical, mental, or emotional, but we can't let those things define who we are or hinder us from pursuing our purpose in life. Some approaches to stuttering try to correct the mechanics of the speech, but in my experience, that approach has limited success. What does work is knowing that your words matter, your ideas matter, and your voice needs to be heard. You have something to say that has value, and you have value. That's why you can't let the discomfort stop you. Today, I'm proud to be working with Dr. Courtney Byrd at the University of Texas at Austin, who shares this perspective, to develop the Arthur M. Blank Center for Stuttering Education and Research, an international research and education institution. It's a disability

that often goes unnoticed, yet it is one that can lead to countless challenges, including bullying, low self-esteem, shame,
depression, and discrimination. Many people who stutter end
up trapped in a limited circle of people and places in which
they feel safe, confined to the words they can say without fear
of stuttering. It's a great loss—to them and to the world.

Bottom line, I didn't let the discomfort stop me or the limita-
tion define me, and I learned to overcome my stutter. Likewise,
both President Carter and I eventually made it to the top of
that cliff, where Rosalynn and our instructor waited patiently.
I was grateful it was over, but even more grateful for what I
learned about myself, once again. I'm capable of more than I
think I am.

Just Enough Tension

As a leader, part of my job is to push people—to create enough
tension in the system that people are not comfortable. It's too
easy for people to fall into routines and get settled in a comfort zone. Leaders need to keep things uncomfortable enough
so that people are constantly asking, "How can I get better?
How can the business do better? What are customers asking
for? What are our competitors doing?" Of course, tension can
get unhealthy if it's not balanced. We want people to be awake,
alert, and on their toes; we don't want them to be anxious, fear-
ful, and overwhelmed. But I've found that people are naturally
inclined to grow when given the impetus and opportunity.

This attitude seems to come naturally to me. I'm always inclined to focus on what more can be done rather than celebrate
what's been achieved. Celebrations are important, of course,

but the more celebrating we do, the bigger the target on our backs. At the original Home Depot headquarters, Bernie and I shared a bathroom between our offices. In the hallway outside the bathroom, we'd hang our press clippings. Not the accolades, the rave reviews, or the awards we'd won, but the negative stories, the criticisms, the failures. And this wasn't just a private ritual—we talked openly about the problems we saw with the company and the things we wanted to improve. When people joined the company from outside, they used to tell us, "If we took what you said literally, we'd think the company was going bankrupt!" When the team at Mountain Sky Guest Ranch tells me that we have a 96 percent return rate—a phenomenal achievement that I celebrate wholeheartedly—I also want to know, what about the other 4 percent? We need to work on that.

At Mercedes-Benz Stadium, we're always focusing on how we can innovate and improve. Although our stadium has ranked number one in food and beverage across all NFL and MLS venues two years in a row, we felt we could still improve, and one area we focused on was the speed of the checkout line. We'd already embraced whole-dollar pricing, which helped speed things up to some extent, but there was no question that cash payments were slow. What if we were to take the whole stadium cashless? Besides improving checkout times, this had the added advantage of giving us more flexibility to lower prices on food items without having to stick to the whole-dollar approach. There were concerns, however. What about fans who didn't have credit cards? Many people argue that cashless businesses disenfranchise lower-income customers who may not have credit or bank accounts (estimated to be about 7 percent of the population). These issues became front-page news in the spring of 2019, when the City of Philadelphia banned cashless businesses. It was a challenge that required a more innovative approach. Excluding any of our fans would have run counter to our values. So we came up with an inclusive solution: we installed "reverse ATMs," which will exchange cash for no-fee debit cards that can be used at our concession stands or anywhere else. Now, with the checkout speed improved, we're turning our attention to how we can get faster and more efficient in other areas of our food service. What we're doing well is great, but what can we do better?

People don't always like this approach in the moment, but they love it in the rearview mirror. Bill Darden, who has project-managed all the major construction projects for our businesses, from our family office to the stadium, has told me that there were numerous times when I pushed him to the brink—"to where I'm about ready to go jump off a bridge or tell you to jump off a bridge." But then, he says, "all of a sudden I'd realize I'm in this incredible place that I didn't realize it was possible to get to." The key is to always push in such a way that you're giving the person a fighting chance of success. It's not just "sink or swim." You can drop someone in the middle of the lake, but you also want to make sure they have a life preserver ready if needed. Knowing that they have that safety device at hand should give them the courage to take more risks. In the midst of the stadium project, when all our associates were stretched almost to their limit, I wanted to remind the executive leadership team of this truth, so I had personalized life preservers made for each them, inscribed with a favorite aphorism: "A ship in harbor is safe, but that is not what ships are built for."

Don't set up people for failure when it can be avoided, or put them in a situation where they simply don't have the training or the skill set to succeed. That's not respectful; it's not putting people first. My goal is always to create a situation that's demanding but contains a high probability of success. And if it becomes clear that the person isn't able to meet the challenge, find a way to move them back, or put them in a role that doesn't require constant growth. Some people need more stability, and an organization needs that kind of person as well.

On occasion, I'll admit, I've pushed people too far. Back in the Home Depot days, there'd come a time of year when managers had to meet with me to get their budgets approved. The accountant in me loved this time of year. For fun, but also to make a point, I would dress all in black for those meetings, and on the table in front of me was a long sword. The message? "If you can't cut your costs, I will do it for you. You need to cut, cut, cut."

One day, our lumber merchant Mike came in. I'd looked over his projections, and I wasn't satisfied. I wanted more sales, more profitability. I told him so.

His response? "I can't give you any more."

I pushed again. "I don't believe you. I need more."

"Look, Arthur," he said, "I can't. I'd give you the shirt off my back. I'll give you everything."

I opened my mouth to push back again, but he interrupted. "Give me a couple of minutes to think about it." So I left the room.

When I came back a few minutes later, I was greeted by a sight I'll never forget. Mike—who was a large man—was lying, nude, on the table. His clothes were piled in front of my seat. He'd certainly made his point!

I'm continually learning when to push and when to ease up, both in my leadership role and in my personal journey. It takes humility to remember that people and organizations can absorb change only at a certain rate. After that you start to undermine their ability to function. If you become too fascinated with the shiny new thing, and the next shiny new thing, you can begin to neglect the people who got you there.

Sometimes I rely on my leadership team to help in this regard. When the stadium was finally finished, in the fall of 2017, we spent a couple of days at an offsite meeting. Steve, our CEO, had a clear message for me: "It's time to get out of startup mode and reinvest in our culture." Steve knew the difference between positive and negative stress, and he was seeing too many signs of the latter. The construction marathon, along with the soccer team launch, had pushed everyone to extremes. The wheels had been wobbling nonstop for more than three years. And we'd made it through. Everyone had gone above and beyond, stepping so far out of their comfort zones they couldn't even see them in the rearview mirror. But if we didn't switch gears, people would burn out and we'd start to lose them. We'd been prioritizing our "innovate continuously" value, but we needed to rebalance it with putting people first.

I heard him. It was a moment to take a deep breath, celebrate our achievements, and let our associates enjoy what they'd built—literally. We started to use the stadium facility for team-building activities and just plain fun. Associates would gather for coffee and donuts at one of the bars, celebrate successes, or organize a field day. All of this helped to boost morale and helped people recharge.

I appreciate the importance of balance, but it's hard for me personally to ever feel settled. That's not to say I don't find great satisfaction and joy in the journey, but my natural inclination is always to keep moving. Perhaps it was losing my father so young that instilled in me a sense of existential urgency. Perhaps it was my mother's determination and drive to succeed. Whatever the reason, I have always lived by a favorite quote from Nike founder Phil Knight: "There is no finish line." I wonder if there ever will be. My eldest daughter, Dena, always tells me, "Dad, that's okay if you're a runner." She wishes that at this stage of my life, I could learn to release some of that pressure. So I'm working on that. Maybe that's the next frontier of innovation, at least on a personal level. But when it comes to business, I'll always believe that there's further to go. As great as things may be, that's all history. We're capable of more.

Chapter 9

Walk in Their Shoes

Leaders volunteer to go first into danger. Their willingness to sacrifice for us is the reason we're inspired to follow.

—SIMON SINEK

In the lobby of our Atlanta offices stands a custom bronze statue of a Sioux warrior in full battle regalia—feathered headdress and shield, fringed leather leggings, black and white war paint. Behind him, a sharpened staff is planted firmly in the ground, decorated from top to bottom with fifty eagle feathers. A leather belt encircles the warrior's waist and attaches to the shaft of the staff. He cannot move from his position on the battlefield—he will stand his ground until victory or death. Chin proudly lifted and eyes scanning the horizon, he raises his bow, an arrow poised on the string.

This work, by one of my favorite artists, Dave McGary, is entitled *Point of No Return,* and it depicts a time-honored tradition of Sioux leadership. Before a battle, a member of the elite Strong Heart Society—the tribe's most fearless warriors— would be selected to establish a position at the front of the battlefield and plant his staff, known as a waving banner, in the ground. There he would stand, unmoving, no matter what the outcome of the fight. To me, this exemplifies what it means to lead by example. That warrior will not ask any of those he leads to take an arrow for him or run ahead of him into danger. He cannot retreat or shield himself behind his troops. What he asks them to do, he is willing to do himself, and do first.

I don't like to think of business as a battlefield, but nevertheless, the warrior's example strikes me as a fitting one for leaders in any business. We should always strive to set an example, not shy away from the difficult tasks or let others take the fall for us. Our associates should feel their leaders are standing with them, not looking down from some corporate HQ.

It's for this reason that every time the Falcons play, I go down to the sideline in the fourth quarter. When there are eight or nine minutes left in the game, I leave my seat and make my way to an area between the goal line and the thirty-five-yard line. I don't interact with the players or interfere with the coaches in any way, but they know I'm there. This is an unusual thing for an NFL owner to do, and even though I've been doing it for almost two decades, the press and the fans of our opponents still misunderstand it, accusing me of drawing attention to myself and not knowing my place. But I really don't care what they say. I do it for our players and coaches. It's my way of telling them, "I'm here with you, shoulder to shoulder, win or lose." When the game goes into crunch time, I'm not going to be up in my suite hobnobbing with VIPs. I don't care if it's freezing cold or a scorching summer day, I'm going to be down here with you.

Sidelined

The third quarter was almost halfway done when Matt Ryan's touchdown pass extended the Falcons' lead over the New England Patriots to a commanding twenty-five points. As I jumped out of my seat with joy, I started to let myself believe that for the first time in Falcons' history, pro football's greatest prize could be within our grasp. After a triumphant season, we'd won the NFC championship and earned our place on the field in Houston for Super Bowl LI on February 5, 2017. I'm never one to declare victory too soon, but anyone who's been around football will tell you that it's almost impossible to lose when you're that far ahead. Never in Super Bowl history had a team made up more than a ten-point deficit to win. ESPN's win probability calculator gave us a 99.6 percent chance at that point in the game. Our defense had held Tom Brady and the Patriots scoreless through most of the first half, and our offense seemed unstoppable.

The Patriots got their first points on the board just before the half, and they rallied toward the end of the third quarter, but we still had a sixteen-point lead when I made my way through the jubilant crowd in our suite and down to the sidelines. Nine minutes to go. I glanced at screens as I hurried down, not wanting to miss a single play. And then it all started to go horribly wrong.

To this day I can't reasonably explain how we went from 28–3 to a tied-up game headed for the first overtime in Super Bowl history, even though I stood as close as one can get to the action and watched it with my own eyes. I can recite from memory the sequence of events—the mistakes, the injuries, the decisions I wish we'd made differently, the calls that went against us, the moments of brilliance, the missed opportunities, the relentless advance of our opponents, and the infamous coin flip. I can still see Julio Jones stretching for that miraculous catch on the twenty-two-yard line that should have turned the tide. And I can feel the thud of Matt Ryan hitting the field as he got sacked and we lost our chance to score. But to add that all up to thirty-one unanswered points for our opponents and the biggest comeback in the history of the sport's biggest game takes an incalculable equation of bad luck and unfortunate choices.

Standing on the sidelines as the final whistle blew, there was no way to avoid the spotlight—or the red, white, and blue confetti that rained down around me. I couldn't take a moment in the privacy of the suite and gather myself before facing the cameras. My disbelief and devastation were captured in thousands of images. I was accused of taking a premature victory lap and even jinxing the team. But that was okay. People didn't understand that I'm always on the sidelines in the fourth quarter, win or lose, and there's nowhere else I would have wanted to be when our team faced its most crushing defeat.

No doubt, by this point, some among you are thinking, "Okay, come on, it's just a game!" And yes, it was just a game. I'll always be the first to remind my associates, my kids, and frequently myself that there are much bigger problems in the world than the loss of a football game or a soccer match. But I also couldn't be in this business if I didn't feel every loss like a punch to my gut and love every win as if it were my first. And there is no bigger win, or loss, than the Super Bowl. Our players, coaches, and support staff; my family; and our fans had invested so much energy and passion in getting us there.

We'd brought every one of our associates and members of their families to Houston for the game. All of them would be reeling from the loss.

As I stood there on the sideline watching the Patriots celebrate while our guys shuffled off the field, I knew that any moment now it would be my job to keep things in perspective for everyone else. It would be my responsibility to make sure that our organization, our players, our coaching staff, and our fans had the resilience to bounce back from this. It would be up to me to set the tone. Everyone would be wondering, "What's the owner going to do? Is he going to go crazy? Is he going to rip into his coach?" I'd need to summon up dignity, maturity, and empathy. But for those few seconds, I just let myself feel the heartbreak.

Making my way through the crush of press and fans and players, I headed to the locker room, as I always do after a game. There was nothing to say; I just gave each of the players a hug. They were all about to face the media, but I had a chance to set the tone first and let them know it was going to be okay. As I was leaving the locker room, I saw a young boy standing to the side, crying. I recognized him as our GM's son, Mason, so I went over and gave him a hug as well. I showed up at our postgame party and was supportive of my family, our associates, and our guests. It was an opportunity, I reminded myself, to show my kids how to deal with adversity in the healthiest way that you can. It had taken me years to learn this myself. When I first bought the team, I would bring losses home with me, retreating from my family until my black mood lifted. But over time I realized that I wasn't setting the right example for my kids. Setbacks are inevitable, in business and in life, and the attitude with which you deal with them is what will define your leadership and your organization over the long term. It's not just a matter of maintaining one's composure; it's a matter of staying true to one's values. These days, I strive to learn from a loss, whether personal or professional—to absorb it, reflect on it, and then move past it.

The immediate aftermath of such a blow is usually a time to take care of people, not a time to crack the whip. As a leader, it's important to know the difference. I was particularly aware that our coach, Dan Quinn, would need my support. There were certainly things we would need to learn and things we would need to change. We beat ourselves in the second half of that game more than the Patriots beat us. The coaching staff made choices they wished they could take back. But right then they needed me to set an example of being positive, looking ahead, learning from our mistakes, and moving on.

Back in Atlanta, there was only one thing to do: get back to work. Everyone was still reeling from the loss, but there was nothing to be gained from sitting in the corner, sucking our thumbs, and feeling sorry for ourselves. If I walked around sulking, everybody else would do the same. An organization's attitude always starts at the top. So, I called a meeting of the executive team that Tuesday.

We gathered in our Kurt Hahn Conference Room, named after the founder of Outward Bound. All our conference rooms are named after my personal heroes, but this one was a particularly appropriate venue for the moment, I reflected, thinking of Hahn's motto, "To strive, to serve, and not to yield." First, I gave everyone a chance to share how they were feeling. It's not healthy to bury those difficult emotions, but neither is it particularly useful to dwell on them. The longer you linger with them, the unhealthier they become. In the wake of a loss or setback, whether it's a football game, a business deal, or a personal failure, there's a tendency to narrowly focus on what went wrong and what could have been. Of course, there's always value in reflecting constructively on what can be learned and what could be done differently next time. But once that's been done, what matters is the big picture. Your long-term goals don't change just because of a short-term stumble or even a crashing fall.

At that meeting, I reminded everyone that all our associates and fans were feeling the same way we were, but they were also looking to us to see how we conducted ourselves. We shouldn't forget that we'd just had our best season ever. We'd won the NFC championship. We had an MVP quarterback and a young team. "I'm going to remember all of that and hold my head up when I leave this room," I told them, "and I expect you to do the same."

Besides, we simply couldn't afford to waste a moment or expend any energy dragging around regrets and recriminations. In exactly thirty days, our soccer team would step onto the pitch for the first time. The stadium was overbudget and behind schedule, and it would take a Herculean effort to ensure that it was ready for the opening of the next NFL season. We had work to do. Lots of it.

So did the Falcons. Everyone talks about the "Super Bowl hangover"—the slump so often seen in teams the year after they fail to win the championship. The press were convinced we would tank. But we proved them wrong. Dan and all our coaching staff did a phenomenal job, the fans lifted us up, and the team got back on the field, made some changes, and went to the playoffs again the following year—the only team in our conference to have done so. We're still chasing that ring, and it still hurts to think about how close we came. In fact, sometimes it hurts more than it did at the time because back then, my focus was on being a role model. I never fully let it hit me. But every year since, when the league gets ready for the big game, I relive that crushing disappointment and wonder if we have what it takes to get there again. I confess, I threw out all my Super Bowl LI gear—it was too painful a reminder. But most of the time, my attention is on the future, and I have great confidence in the commitment and resilience of our team.

Let's Take a Walk

Leading by example is particularly important when confronting a crisis or setback, but it's also something that must be done on a daily basis, in countless small ways. As leaders, we're always setting an example through our actions, whether we're aware of it or not, and one of the most important examples a leader can set is that of being willing to serve. We often hear the phrase *servant leadership* in business these days, but how literally do we take it? If you're a leader or a manager, ask yourself this: When was the last time you directly interacted with your company's customers? When was the last time you personally delivered a product or service, answered a question, or listened to a complaint? When was the last time you saw a problem and just fixed it yourself?

If you're just getting started in business, it's much more likely that the answer to those questions is "Today!" In the early days of a startup, the founders often do everything. In the early Home Depot days, Bernie and I offloaded merchandise, stacked shelves, and served customers alongside everyone else. When the first store opened, our cardboard compactors—the machines we use to crush the packaging that all the merchandise arrives in—were not delivered on time. There was a growing mountain of cardboard at the back of the store, filling up the receiving area where we were supposed to offload new merchandise. So when the compactors finally arrived, I went straight to the back of the store and spent a whole day and most of the night running that machine.

At a certain point, one of the associates went to the store manager and said, "I don't know who this guy is at the back of the store, but he's been back on that compactor for twenty-four hours and he hasn't stopped!"

The store manager told him, "He's one of the owners of the business." The associate thought he was kidding.

That's the kind of example I always want to set. Too often, as a company grows and scales, and as leaders climb the so-called corporate ladder, it takes them further and further away from the beating heart of the business. It may not be practical or desirable in a large company for the owner to spend all day running a compactor, working behind the checkout, or answering customer questions, but there are always ways for a leader to stay connected to the customer and to the act of service, and in so doing to set an example for associates and communicate that everyone is in it together. These opportunities are priceless and should be sought out whenever possible. Ideally, people shouldn't feel as if they're working *for* you; they should feel as if they're working *with* you. And nothing sends that message as clearly as actually showing up beside them from time to time and rolling up your sleeves.

That's not to say that delegation isn't a critical leadership skill or that managers should get overinvolved in every detail of a business. But a leader should never lose their direct connection to the people they're serving or to the associates who interact with those people every day. If your company values are really about service to others, then no one—from the leader on down—should hesitate to serve. Don't ask any associate to perform a task you wouldn't do yourself. No job is beneath you when it comes to taking care of the people you work with and the people you serve—in fact, the very concept of "beneath" makes no sense when you invert the management pyramid and put service at the top.

As The Home Depot grew and we could no longer spend every day in the aisles, Bernie and I made sure to tour the country to visit our growing number of stores and do regular "store walks." Often, these walks took several hours, partly because the stores were so big but also because customers would stop us to ask questions. Where can I find carpet shampoo? What's the best brand of sealant? Would these floor tiles work in my kids' bathroom? They had no idea who we were—we never wore suits when we visited stores, and we always tied on orange aprons so we looked just like every other associate. We'd take a detour from our walks to guide customers to the right shelves and do our best to advise them on the merchandise, or find someone who knew more than we did, which was never too hard to do. It also gave us a chance to personally thank our customers for their support.

I still do store walks today whenever I visit one of our PGA TOUR Superstore locations. I love checking out what Dick Sullivan and his team are doing in each store. And I'll interrupt our walk to ask a lost-looking customer if they need help finding something or to answer a question. I sometimes see the associates who are hosting me glance anxiously at the clock when the two-hour tour turns into three or four hours. But I know they're also getting an important message: the owner thinks the customers are more important than anybody else. We're a service business, and I'm going to serve right along-side you. There's nothing more critical I could communicate to them as a leader, and I look for any opportunity to reinforce that message, not just through my words but through my actions. I know I'm not the only one delivering that message; the company's entire leadership team empties out of their Store Support Center and works on the store floors during key selling periods, such as Father's Day.

One way that we've instituted this attitude across our businesses today is through a program we call Walk in My Shoes. The idea is simple: get people out of the offices and give them the direct experience of serving our customers, guests, and fans. For example, all our support associates in Atlanta will be assigned to spend a shift working in a frontline service role at the stadium on an event day. Our fans don't know it, but the guy flipping burgers might be the team president. The woman checking tickets could be the head of our foundation. The person they ask for directions to their seats could be the same person who was responsible for keeping the stadium construction on schedule.

This program is not about observing the work; it's about actually doing the work, alongside those who do it every day. There are several reasons this is important. It communicates to associates that their leaders don't consider it beneath them to serve. It keeps office staff connected to the fans, guests, and customers the business is serving. And it's also a source of invaluable feedback and innovation. A frontline associate might not complain about a badly designed system or process. They make the best of it. But when their leaders see and work with those systems and processes for themselves, they know what needs to change. Our switch to a self-service soda station, back at the Georgia Dome, came as a result of Falcons president Rich McKay taking a shift at the soda stand and realizing just how inefficient it was to pour fans' drinks one by one.

For a recent Walk in My Shoes day, the CEO of our for-profit businesses, Steve Cannon, worked a concession stand at Mercedes-Benz Stadium during one of our busiest events of the year. At our next executive leadership team meeting, it was one of the main things he spoke about.

"Even if you walk past a thing a thousand times, don't make the mistake of thinking you understand it," he said.

He meant that quite literally. Steve walks the concourses before every single event—it's part of his pregame ritual. But as he shared that day, even though he's passed those concession stands for years, greeting the associates who work there, thanking them, checking out what's on the menu, it wasn't until he actually tied on an apron and worked alongside them that he truly understood what they were dealing with. It was a fine operation, he said, but there were countless small things that didn't work as well as they could and should. One example he shared with us involved french fries. The kitchen in the back would load the fries into their cartons and put them in a chute, where they could slide down to the servers in the front. The problem, however, was that the package design was top-heavy, and at least 50 percent of the cartons would fall over as they moved down the chute. Steve felt terrible handing customers half-portions while so much food was going to waste on the floor. So he challenged our food and beverage partner to redesign the system. To his great delight, not long afterward, he received a video showing full carton after full carton of french fries smoothly making their way down a new and improved chute.

Our leaders don't restrict their Walk in My Shoes shifts to officially scheduled times. One night between back-to-back events, the stadium cleanup crew was looking overwhelmed, so Rich McKay decided to step in and help. One of the first things he noticed was that they didn't have enough pressure washers to do the job, so an associate was dispatched to the nearest Home Depot store to pick up some more. When the pressure washers arrived, Rich got behind one, and pretty soon he made a decision on the spot: no more peanuts. The mess those shells made—falling down between the seats, getting stuck in every crack, clogging up the drains—was unmanageable. Rich said he sure as hell didn't want to deal with them again, and why should any of our associates? So we stopped selling them. I don't think the fans miss them too much, and the team that does that job after every event was delighted. But we might never have made that change if Rich hadn't been the one manning the pressure washer that night.

When I first bought the Falcons, I did an unofficial Walk in My Shoes at our very first training camp. In those days, the team used to rent facilities up at Furman University. It's a really nice college with a pretty campus, and when the university president heard that I was planning to come to camp, he called me up to let me know he'd reserved a house for me, right down the street from his own home. I thanked him but told him that wouldn't be necessary—I'd be staying with the players and coaches on campus. He tried to convince me I'd be more comfortable in the house, but my mind was made up. As a new owner, I needed to understand the players' experience directly and to let them know I was in this with them.

What struck me the moment I walked into my assigned dorm room was that these facilities were made for college kids, not adult football players. I'm six feet tall, and I found the beds too short, so I could only imagine what our players were experiencing. I later learned that many opted to take the mattress off the bed and sleep on it on the floor. The shower heads were also far too small, and the towels were tiny. No one complained, but it was far from ideal. Plus, very few fans showed up to watch the team training because it was a long drive from Atlanta.

As a result of attending that training camp, when it came to building new player housing at our own facility, I invited a group of players to sit down with the architect and design their own rooms, amenities, and so on—right down to the size of the beds, shower heads, and towels. I had already decided we would build our own place, but if I hadn't actually taken a walk in those very large shoes, I might not have really understood what the players needed. Those small changes made a huge difference.

When we're hiring people to work in our businesses, particularly in leadership roles, we always look for this willingness and ability to put themselves in the shoes of those they'll be leading. On the whole, we've been successful, and I like to think we have many servant leaders on our team. But there have also been instances when we've gotten it wrong. Bobby Petrino was one of those. In 2006, the Falcons were looking for a new head coach, and his incredible track record at the University of Louisville caught the attention of our organization. We flew up to meet him, and when the meeting was over, my team told me, "You've got to make a decision right away." If word got out that he'd taken the meeting, they explained, Petrino would be fired by the college, so we had to move fast.

I was taken aback—I never like to rush decisions when it comes to people. I take the time to get to know someone and get a feel for whether they're aligned with our values. But in this case, I wanted to respect the collective wisdom of the football operations staff, and I let myself be pressured into a hasty choice. And I'd soon regret it. It's very rare for players to call me directly, but a couple of our players did just that in the weeks that followed. The essence of their message: "Who the hell did you hire?" When I inquired further, I found out that the new coach was treating the men on our team like college kids—acting like a tough guy, setting arbitrary rules, such as no television during mealtimes. He seemed to have no ability to work with mature adults, and he never really connected with the team. Not only was he refusing to walk in their shoes, it was as if he were insisting they wear his shoes.

Not surprisingly, this story had an unhappy ending. Things came to a head when we were scheduled to play on *Monday Night Football,* and I knew I'd be asked on live television how our coach was doing. I met with Petrino and asked him directly where his heart was at and what he'd want me to say. We had what seemed to me to be a good conversation about some of his frustrations, and at the end of it he shook my hand and said, "You tell them that you have a coach." So I did. What I didn't know was that he'd already planned his exit. There was a plane from the University of Arkansas waiting for him the next day, and he boarded it without even saying goodbye, to take a job as their new head coach. I only fully understood

what had happened when I was sitting in bed later that night
and saw him giving a press conference and doing the team's
famous "hog call" cheer, surrounded by cheerleaders. It was
a surreal ending to a difficult chapter for the Falcons, and a
lasting lesson for me.

Interestingly, the following year, when we were looking for
a new quarterback, we did an on-campus workout with one of
Petrino's former players from Louisville. After the workout, he
took me aside. "Mr. Blank," he said politely, "do you mind if I
ask you something?"

"Sure," I replied.

"What possessed you to hire Bobby Petrino?" he asked.
"Anyone who played with him could have told you he couldn't
coach adults."

I had no good answer for him, other than that I'd failed to follow my values and my instincts in making that decision. It was
a mistake I would not make again when hiring for such a critical role. After Petrino left, we began the search for a new head
coach and a general manager, and to my surprise, I received
a rare email from my Home Depot cofounder Bernie Marcus,
who I always joke doesn't know how to use a computer. "Keep
in mind how we hired people at The Home Depot," he wrote.
"First and foremost based on character, integrity, and trust."

It was a timely reminder. Another way to put it would be:
hire for culture. Choose someone based on whether they'll
be a good cultural fit and contribute to the company's expression of its values. It's for this reason that it's always been my
policy to conduct several interviews: some formal and some
informal; some with multiple people present and others that
are one-on-one. You often learn more about a candidate over a
lunch or dinner where the conversation is about their family

and their hobbies than you do in an office interview focused on their qualifications and work experience. And if you meet with the person a number of times, you're likely to pick up on any characteristics or attitudes that might not fit well with your culture. Besides Petrino, the one other significant hire that did not go through this lengthy process was Nardelli. In both cases, I believe that had we been less rushed in our decisions, we might not have ultimately made the mistakes we did.

When seeking Petrino's replacement, I let the football experts focus on the football side of things and I focused all my attention on the person. Was he trustworthy? Did he have character? Was he a team player? Was he willing to learn to grow? The resulting hires turned out to be pivotal for us: Thomas Dimitroff, who is still our general manager more than a decade later, and Coach Mike Smith, or Smitty as he was known, who delivered the Falcons their first-ever back-to-back winning seasons—not just two but five. They were both experts in the craft, but more importantly they were great cultural fits for our franchise. And that meant they were leaders who walked their talk. In the end, there's nothing more important in a leader than a willingness to lead by example.

||||||||||||

Chapter 10

From Protest to Progress

We are united . . . by a common history and heritage—by
a respect for the deeds of the past and a recognition of the
needs of the future. Never satisfied with today, we have
always staked our fortunes on tomorrow. . . .

   This country is moving and it must not stop. It cannot
stop. For this is a time for courage and a time for challenge.
Neither conformity nor complacency will do.

—PRESIDENT JOHN F. KENNEDY, FROM THE
SPEECH HE WAS DUE TO GIVE ON THE DAY OF
HIS ASSASSINATION, NOVEMBER 22, 1963

As a kid, I wanted to be Jackie Robinson when I grew up.
To this day, some of my most cherished memories are of going with my dad to watch the Brooklyn Dodgers play ball. We
would take a bus and two subways, hop off at Prospect Park,
hang a right, and there she stood: Ebbets Field.

I was there to cheer on my boys, Roy Campanella, Duke
Snider, Pee Wee Reese. And Jackie. We usually sat in the upper
deck. Hot dog vendors in brown aprons and paper hats hawked
their wares: "Franks, twenty cents!" Eyes peeped through
whittled-out knotholes in the outfield fence. Men wore hats
and sport coats; the ladies, skirt suits and pumps. I wanted one

of those Dodger-blue Bowery Boys caps, a wool felt beanie with "Dodgers" primitively stitched in white, but that was beyond our means. The organ played "Take Me Out to the Ball Game." Local Little League players (lucky dogs) took to the diamond and warmed up alongside the pros against a backdrop of ads for cigarettes, shoe polish, and wrinkle-proof ties.

The stadium (or "band box," as it was affectionately known) held about thirty-two thousand fans max, the smallest in the National League. Fans sat virtually atop the players. When Jackie ran, we all ran. When Pee Wee dove, we all hit the dirt. If the Dodgers won, we went home with a spring in our step and rejoiced. If our boys lost, we mourned, then moved on, knowing they needed us to pull our heads out of our moping asses to cheer them on twice as hard the next game. We were in it together, win or die.

I wasn't in the stands on April 15, 1947, when Jackie took a small step up to the plate and a giant leap over the color line, becoming the first African American in Major League Baseball since 1884. Even if I had been, at four years old I'd have been too young to understand the epic significance of that moment. That guy wasn't supposed to swing for the bleachers, but he did. And he hushed everyone in the crowd—naysayer and fan alike—through his undeniable excellence. With the backing of Dodgers president and GM Branch Rickey, Jackie made history, and within a couple of years, he was followed by three-time MVP Roy Campanella, Don Newcombe, Jim Gilliam, and Joe Black.

By the time I was scrambling up the bleachers to my seat in the top deck, clutching my popcorn and grinning from ear to ear, it seemed almost normal that the team had black players and white players, just as the stadium was filled with a diversity of fans. Yet just a few years earlier, opposing teams had yelled racial slurs and pitchers had aimed at Jackie's head. And in much of the country, in the early 1950s, the battle for desegregation and civil rights was just getting started.

Growing up in a very inclusive household and a diverse community, I didn't encounter these tensions directly. I couldn't name the deep history and vast cultural forces that made what Jackie, Branch Rickey, and the Dodgers had done such a big deal. But I felt it in my gut. Perhaps it was partly my Jewish heritage and the legacy of my immigrant grandparents. Perhaps it was partly because I was a kid who spoke with a stutter and was maliciously picked on for it. Whatever the reason, Jackie's every success resonated with me. I'd hold my breath along with every other fan in the stands as he inched out, every muscle tensed, trying to steal a base. He inspired a lifelong commitment to rooting for the underdog that still influences everything I do today.

It's an understatement to note that professional sports always have been and remain a potent litmus test of what moves and shakes us as a country. I did not step into the NFL thinking I would encounter challenges even remotely like those that Branch Rickey and Jackie Robinson had faced seven decades earlier. We live in vastly different times, thanks in large part to heroes like them. But in the years that I have owned the Falcons, the NFL has become a stage, again and again, for some of the toughest questions we're facing as a nation today. The Falcons and all our businesses have been forced to ask ourselves these questions: How will we participate in this moment in history? How can we, as a team and as a business, respond to these momentous issues with grace and diplomacy?

In these polarized times, it's not just sports franchises that must ask these questions. Any business can unexpectedly find itself balancing precipitously over a cultural fault line. Starbucks ended up in the hot seat over racial profiling just a few years ago, when an employee called the cops on two black men who were simply waiting for a friend in one of its Philadelphia stores. Google found itself grappling with issues of gender and diversity after a now infamous memo from an engineer went viral. Every social media company is compelled to grapple with privacy and free speech. Do all these companies handle such moments well? Let's just say some do better than others. Not all leaders in business or professional sports feel inclined to prioritize the rights of others over the operations of their business. But like it or not, we are all realizing the same fundamental truth: we no longer live in a world where business can keep itself separate from social and political concerns. I for one think that's a good thing, and I'm proud that our businesses continue to work proactively to find values-driven solutions that address the forces at the very root of these issues. Wherever possible, the job of a leader is to find a way to move the company—and in some cases, the broader circles of society around it—from protest to progress.

Take a Knee

During the 2016 preseason, when Colin Kaepernick and a handful of other players took a knee during the national anthem to protest police brutality and racism, it created a stir in the league, though initially it was fairly small. Some fans felt that in refusing to stand during the anthem, these players were disrespecting the flag that, to them, symbolized our military, with which the NFL and our fans have a close relationship. Of course, the protests had nothing to do with the military, and most servicemen and -women we spoke to seemed to know that. Our CEO, Steve Cannon, is a West Point graduate, and he made it clear that from his perspective, the players were exercising the very rights he had served to protect. Nonetheless, some fans were angry, along with some key sponsors. Personally, I felt that the players were within their rights and the issues they were raising were important ones. They were also complex ones, with tangled histories that would not be easily smoothed out. America has a proud tradition of protest, and these men were making a conscious decision to risk their livelihoods in order to make a social statement, on the most public platform that they had available. I respected that.

One of my contemporary heroes is the lawyer and activist Bryan Stevenson, the author of *Just Mercy*, who writes and speaks about the mass incarceration crisis today and its connection to this country's history of slavery and racism. A powerful lesson I've learned from Bryan is the importance of acknowledging and affirming the truth of that history and its continuing manifestations. We have to be willing to stop, look it right in the face, and say, "Yes. This is what took place, and this is what is taking place." Too many of us want to skip over that uncomfortable truth and start looking for solutions without really *being with* the reality of the problem. In so doing, even with the best of intentions, we continue to perpetuate the marginalization of those who are victimized—their sense of being unseen and unheard. So when I saw players kneeling in protest, just like when people in the Westside communities expressed resistance to our stadium plans, I reminded myself that they had every reason to be doing so. These injustices are taking place today, in our streets, our courts, our prisons. Police shootings. Mass incarceration. Mandatory minimums on prison sentences. Yes, we've come a long way from the dark days of slavery and segregation. Yet we still have real racial issues in this country.

I'd like to find a way to move us all toward collaborative solutions, but first we need to fully acknowledge and understand the problems. It comes back to one of our core values: listen and respond. You can't effectively respond before you've truly listened. You can't create a win-win until you admit that some people have been on the losing side. You can't get to progress before you affirm the reasons for protest.

The anthem protests escalated sharply in September 2017 after certain inflammatory remarks were made by President Trump at a rally in Huntsville, Alabama. Suddenly, outraged players across the country began joining the protests, with more than three hundred choosing to take a knee the weekend after those remarks were made. Owners were pressured to crack down, and some did. Sponsors threatened to withdraw their support. Angry fans stayed away from games. TV ratings fell. I watched in growing concern as our league became the stage for a divisive drama. Making this about patriotism didn't solve anything. The issues the players were raising were real and needed to be talked about. That would itself be a patriotic act, one that strengthened our nation. Polarizing the issue didn't help.

We were scheduled to play in Detroit a couple days later, and it was possible that some on our team would feel compelled to protest. We had already begun a dialogue with our players, giving them a forum in which they could tell us what mattered to them and express how they felt about the issues, and we could all start a conversation about how we were going to face this, together. We knew the difficult position they found themselves in. Close to 70 percent of players in the league are African American, and as you can imagine, many of them were getting calls from family telling them that that Sunday they were *going* to take a knee. Parents and grandparents who had marched in the streets were telling the next generation: it's your turn now.

On the sidelines before the Detroit game, I spoke with the Lions owner, Martha Ford, then ninety-two years old. She asked me how I planned to handle the situation.

"Well," I said, "what they do is their choice. I'm not going to tell our players not to kneel. And I'm not going to punish them for expressing themselves. I'm supportive of their rights to express their freedom of speech." I wanted to do something visible to show my commitment and understanding. So I'd decided, after talking to the coaching staff, to stay down on the field for the anthem and to stand and link arms with the players and coaches. Mrs. Ford decided she would do the same. Two of our players did kneel, and the rest stood, their arms linked.

The next day, as they always do on the Monday after a game, the players gathered for a meeting. There was no talk of football. Instead, the players who had knelt spoke honestly and vulnerably about why. Grady Jarrett, our defensive tackle, declared that he just could not tolerate the slur the president had used to describe them. "I'm not a son of a bitch, I'm the son of a queen!" he had told reporters after the game.[1] At the meeting, he described his everyday experience of racism in such vivid terms that none who were present will forget it.

There was no question that we needed to respond to these issues in real, tangible ways. Symbolic gestures on the field were all well and good, but if we were to move beyond these protests rather than simply shut them down, what we really needed was progress on the issues themselves. Our foundation was already engaged in work on the Westside, which included initiatives around policing and racial discrimination, but I saw an opportunity to more deeply connect the Falcons players to that work and to inspire a greater engagement with social justice throughout the league. So when the NFL set about convening a committee to tackle the issue, I was asked to serve, along with several other owners.

We sat down together—several owners; the commissioner, Roger Goodell, and other league executives; and a number of players and retired players—and we had a productive initial conversation about their areas of concern. I was deeply impressed with the players who were present—the breadth of their knowledge of the issues at stake; the vulnerability with which they described their own experience and those of their families and friends; the depth of their commitment to lasting change. For our part, as owners and league executives, we made sure the players knew that we understood the magnitude of their concerns and that they were not going to be solved overnight. However, we intended to use the significant platform we had as a league to move things in the right direction. And we as a committee spent most of our time listening.

Most NFL players are not shy about voicing their opinions. They made it clear that for them, this had nothing to do with the military or the flag. This was about specific issues: law-enforcement accountability; curbing poverty; reforming bail-bond laws and regulations; and stepping up community involvement. What was clear was that the players wanted to know we'd be in the ring with them, shoulder to shoulder, not just cheering them on from the corner. They recognized that as owners we had both resources and connections to lawmakers and other political influencers at the state and federal levels who could help move the needle on matters of policy.

One of the key understandings that came out of that meeting is that the issues are not necessarily the same across the country. They vary by state, in terms of laws, cultural attitudes, demographics, economics, and so on. Many of our players grew up in communities where these issues are all too real for their families and friends, and they know what it's like in those streets. They may now be making enough money to have moved to a better neighborhood, but they still go back to visit, and they see the problems firsthand. So they asked us to pay attention to the issues at a local level. This gave rise to the idea of developing social justice action committees for each club, where the players would be the members. To guide the focus of these local efforts, the Players Coalition came up with three broad areas of concern: criminal justice reform, police/community relations, and education and economic advancement.

Back home, we launched the Atlanta Falcons Social Justice Initiative. Our family foundation and the Falcons community relations team got involved to support them in implementing their ideas. The players put together their own set of initiatives that specifically addressed their areas of concern. These included mentoring youth in underserved neighborhoods, strengthening relationships between the community and law enforcement, improvements in officer training, programs to help ex-offenders find employment, and much more. We got involved in advocating for key criminal justice reforms in our state. I personally participated in police drive-alongs, and even took my son Max with me one time so that he too could see first-hand what an officer has to deal with. It was an eye-opening experience, to say the least. In the midst of the cultural reckoning with the tragic consequences of police overreach, it was also an important reminder of the bravery of the officers who put themselves in harm's way to keep our communities safe.

I still serve on the league's social action committee today. We've made a good start in addressing the issues that inspired the process, and we've committed a lot of resources to continuing that work. And there's a long way to go. The divisiveness that characterizes political discourse in our country today seems constantly to threaten to undo our work. But we're dedicated. I think the players today do understand, appreciate, and acknowledge that there is a commitment in the league to work together on these issues in a collaborative way. And we all know that the issues we're addressing are not going to go away overnight. It's going to take time, but we're making progress.

From Crisis Management to Growth Opportunity

It's become something of a cliché that every crisis holds an opportunity, but I do believe it to be true. And one of the opportunities we found in the anthem protest crisis was to put our core values into practice. Every one of our values came into play during that time. We respected our players and their concerns more than we worried about lost revenue or clamoring sponsors. We ensured that all key stakeholders were around the table and involved in the initiatives—the players, the league, but also local community members, law enforcement officials, and government. We were learning as we went, willing to try new things and change course if needed. We saw ourselves as a prototype for what other teams might do. We even produced materials detailing our approach, which we shared with the league. And we approached the entire affair not as a crisis to be managed but as an opportunity to give something to the players who made our sport what it is and to our communities.

Every company has moments when uncomfortable issues suddenly surface and disrupt business-as-usual. They may not play out on national television in front of tens of millions of viewers, but nevertheless, they shake up everyone involved. No company wants to become the stage for the next morality play, and in this social media age, it's all too easy for that to happen. When any organization becomes a microcosm of national or even global tensions, it's important to have the humility to know the scope of the forces you're dealing with. Oftentimes, the issues at stake and the emotions attached to them are much greater than the particular incident. It can feel like your company is taking the fall for conflicts that far transcend its walls. But just because they're bigger than you or your company doesn't mean you're off the hook when it comes to contributing to progress.

To be clear, I'm not saying a company or its leaders should simply bow to the online mob or jump to publicly apologize for every perceived infraction of political correctness. But I am saying that in these turbulent times, we all need to be willing to take an honest look at ourselves and strive to be more inclusive, more respectful, and more open to seeing the perspectives of others. And we need to have the humility to grapple with big issues, no matter how small or imperfect our response. No single person or company can solve problems like racism or gender discrimination or climate change, and meaningful change doesn't happen overnight. But you can make a difference.

Every business leader and company has a platform, large or small, and there are times when it's appropriate to use that platform for more than just promoting your brand and selling your products or services. In 2003, I found myself in such a position. I was chairing the Metro Atlanta Chamber of Commerce when the incoming Georgia governor, Sonny Perdue, proposed that Georgians be allowed to vote on the reinstatement of the 1956 state flag, which included the Confederate battle flag. We had a series of meetings with the governor and other legislators, as well as business and civic groups, but this approach of quiet diplomacy did not get us very far.

The last thing I wanted was to alienate the new governor by taking a more public stand against him. That could be damaging for our businesses and philanthropic activities. But this was a matter of principle. The flag was a reprehensible symbol of slavery and segregation, and from my perspective, even allowing the question to go on the ballot was unacceptable. So I spoke out as a representative of the Atlanta business community, and we were successful. I was glad I took a stand. As my mother would say, you do the right thing for the right reasons, and you live with the consequences.

When you find yourself in the spotlight of history, don't let short-term fears stop you from doing the right thing. Acknowledge the issue. Don't skip over it. Listen. Bring everyone involved into the conversation. Take meaningful action and try new things. Be transparent, and let others in your industry know about what you're doing. And don't let it drop the minute the spotlight moves to someone else. Staying committed will build trust with your associates and customers, and in the long term, trust is the most valuable currency in business.

Making Room for Redemption

The day our players knelt on the field was not the first time I'd encountered protests in my tenure as the Falcons' owner. In the summer of 2007, on one of the worst days of my long career in business and sports, I arrived at our training facility to find red paint spattered like blood on the gates, and people holding placards with graphic images of suffering dogs. Our star quarterback, Michael Vick—Atlanta's local hero, the burgeoning future face of the NFL, and someone with whom I'd enjoyed a good relationship—had been indicted for his involvement in an illegal dogfighting ring.

We'd first heard rumors that Michael might be involved in dogfighting some weeks earlier, but it was unclear at that point whether there was any substance to the claims. We'd begun an investigation, and I'd called Michael into my office immediately and asked him outright, "Did you do it? Is it true?"

"No, Mr. B.," he assured me. He made the same declaration to the commissioner. For a while, it seemed as though it might be nothing more than gossip, and I gave Michael the benefit of the doubt. I understood that the press too often wanted to believe the worst. And I knew Michael—or at least, I thought I did. I believed him to be a man of his word. I left on vacation, having been assured that the claims were soon to be dropped and there was nothing to worry about.

I was on my flight home when the news reached me, via a

message from the pilot. Michael had confessed and been indicted, and the extent of his involvement in the sordid underworld of dogfighting was far greater than anyone imagined. As I read the stories, I felt sick to my stomach. An animal lover and devoted dog owner, I was appalled by the descriptions of the cruelty that had been uncovered. Michael's fingerprints were on everything, even down to the abhorrent act of executing dogs that did not perform. As the plane began its descent toward Atlanta and the inevitable hordes of waiting press, I sat in a state of stunned disbelief.

I'd been close to Michael. Some had even criticized me for being too close. Traditionally, NFL owners and coaching staff hold a hard line when it comes to any kind of personal relationship with the players, and I respect their reasons for this. However, for me, "Put People First" means treating people as people. If I can't get to know our players; learn about their passions, their histories, their families, and their hopes; and help them in any way that I can, there wouldn't be a reason for me to own a team. I'm always sensitive to what's appropriate, but I won't treat our players like commodities. When Michael came to me for advice on issues like starting a foundation or becoming a father, I tried to offer him the best mentorship I could. He visited our home on several occasions and always took the time to play video games with Josh, who looked up to him. So I felt deeply disappointed and betrayed—both personally and for the franchise—when Michael's shadow life came to light.

From the moment I stepped off that plane, I fielded hundreds of questions from reporters, animal rights activists, sponsors, and fans. But no question was as difficult as the one that came from my son Josh, then ten years old: "Daddy, why would Michael do this?"

Why? That was the question that no one but Michael could answer, and at that moment I don't think he could have answered it truthfully himself. It is my observation that today, with the benefit of hindsight and maturity, he has a greater understanding of the complex mix of personal choices and economic and cultural forces that led him down such a reprehensible path. At the time, the explanation he gave me was striking both for its honesty and for everything it lacked.

"I never thought I'd get caught," he admitted. If Michael had gotten a speeding ticket, someone would just "take care of it," because of who he was. Young superstar athletes are too often told they're invincible, untouchable. Couple that giddy sense of sudden entitlement with the still-powerful momentum of an upbringing in one of the country's poorest and most crime-ridden neighborhoods, and you can start to see where a talented kid like Michael goes off the rails. Intergenerational habits and attitudes are hard to break, and the bonds of family and community run deep. Don't get me wrong—I in no way intend to excuse or rationalize the terrible actions he took, and I will never be able to comprehend how any human being could treat animals with such cruelty. But I do, ongoingly, seek to understand why.

In the wake of the charges against Michael, the Falcons were reeling. Both on and off the field, he was the heart of the team. We were winning games and finally becoming part of the fabric of Atlanta. And the city could not have been prouder of our African American quarterback—still something of a rarity in the league at the time. Michael's fall from grace, with all its undertones of racial and social tension, was nothing short of an existential crisis for our team, our organization, and our brand.

As an organization, we decided immediately that the only way forward was to be transparent and forthright with the press and our fans. We didn't try to distance ourselves from the situation or hole up and wait for the outcome of the trial. We called a press conference, acknowledged everything we knew, and expressed our horror at the crimes. In such moments, transparency is always the best policy, and waiting seldom helps. It took us some time to recover—we lost fans and season ticket holders for a couple of years afterward—but most fans appreciated that we were struggling to deal with the revelations, just as they were.

As the team began the season without their quarterback, Michael pled guilty and was convicted. He served about eighteen months in prison, paid large fines, and was forced to declare bankruptcy. The team ended his contract and recouped a portion of his signing bonus, as was appropriate. His time as a Falcon was over, but personally, I wasn't ready to turn my back on him, however disturbing his actions were to me. I believe in redemption and second chances, and I wanted to give him the opportunity to show that he had learned from his terrible mistakes and changed. I still sensed that he was, at his core, a good man who'd made bad choices but could turn himself around. To be able to inspire people in life and work, a leader has to be able to see each of them as more than one action in one moment. Individual humans are caught in an ongoing historical process, attached to cultural, economic, and political truths that shape who they are. They are also possessed of the power to choose, to change the course of their own lives and those around them. I strive to take both of these truths into account in my own life and my relationships, personal and professional.

After Michael served his time and was released on house

arrest, I went to visit him, taking dinner to his family from his favorite restaurant, Stoney River. He struck me immediately as a more mature and humble man. He told me about his time in prison and about what it had felt like to be stripped of all his wealth and privilege. I left that dinner feeling hopeful that he would go on to live a very different life.

He has. In the decade since his release, Michael has dedicated himself to the cause of animal rights, working with the Humane Society, and he's also toured the country speaking to kids about the power of the choices they make, both good and bad. He's a changed man, and that's why I was proud to welcome him as our guest and honoree when the Falcons played our last regular season game at the Georgia Dome in 2017. For the most part, our fans seemed to feel the same way, giving him a standing ovation.

But redemption is never an easy road. Hundreds of thousands of people signed petitions protesting Michael's selection as a captain for the NFL's 2019 Pro Bowl. The league, I'm glad to say, did not bow to this pressure. I respect and honor the right to protest, and I acknowledge that the fight for animal rights is still active and ongoing in this country and around the world. But I'm also a great believer in progress. And when I see progress made—whether on a societal level or on an individual level—it's more important to acknowledge and support that progress than to keep punishing the original ill.

A Night to Remember

January 31 was Jackie Robinson's birthday. "My childhood hero would have been one hundred years old today," I thought, as I stepped up to the microphone and looked out at the leaders in my own sport—NFL owners, executives, and sponsors. "Welcome to Atlanta."

A couple of days later, the 2019 Super Bowl—professional football's highlight of the season—would be played at Mercedes-Benz Stadium. When the New England Patriots and the Los Angeles Rams stepped onto the field in front of seventy thousand cheering fans and tens of millions of television viewers, it would be all about the game. But at this traditional owners' dinner, as in many of the other events leading up to the game, we were taking the opportunity to do something a little different. The NFL had come to our city, and as hosts, we wanted to share with them what truly makes our city great. We didn't want them just to remember a magnificent stadium, great food, and fancy parties. We wanted them to remember Atlanta's diversity and the extraordinary people who fought, and in some cases died, for civil rights. In the wake of the racial issues we'd been working to address as a league, this felt particularly relevant. We wanted our guests to know that they were stepping into a continuum of history and that we, as an organization and as a city, were proud of that history and committed to continuing to fight for human rights and social justice.

Ever since we won the bid to host Super Bowl LIII, this vision had been taking shape in my mind and heart. The week's events had included a tour of Dr. King's home and his church, Ebenezer Baptist, where we heard from his daughter Bernice and from the church's brilliant young pastor, Reverend Dr. Raphael Gamaliel Warnock. The owners' party was held in a tent on the grounds of the National Center for Civil and Human Rights, and before entering the party, guests walked through the museum's powerful exhibits. Seated on either side of me at the dinner were two civil rights heroes, Ambassador Andrew Young and Representative John Lewis. Three of Dr. King's children, Bernice, Dexter, and MLK III, also attended. We were blessed with a moving performance by John Legend and a stirring collaboration between the choirs from the Temple and Ebenezer Baptist Church. And we had invited someone to be our MC for the evening who represented our core message of inclusion, progress, and redemption. He was not a natural speaker, and I later heard that he showed up early and rehearsed all day to get his speech right. But when Michael Vick stepped up to the microphone, the poignancy of the moment was not lost on anyone in the room.

The night was everything I hoped it would be, and many owners told me afterward how affected they were by the visit. I hope it left everyone who attended with a deeper awareness of our shared history, which still lives on in our culture today. I hope that the next time they face issues relating to fairness and social justice in their businesses, or find themselves confronted by protests, they'll connect the dots to that history and find both strength and inspiration. I hope they'll see efforts at promoting diversity and inclusion not as a box to be checked by HR but as a sacred duty for everyone in the organization to uphold. Because our diversity is our strength—as teams, as companies, and as a country.

I ended my remarks that night with a quote from Dr. King that is now part of his memorial in Washington: "We must come to see that the end we seek is a society at peace with itself, a society that can live with its conscience." None of us can afford to turn away—from the shameful chapters of our history or their continuing ripples in our present—if we as individuals, as organizations, and as a society are to be able to live with our own conscience. It's not always easy to confront the uncomfortable truths of our past or our present. But when we take a good long look at our history, what we also realize is how far we've come. In the same moment that we acknowledge the work that is left to do, we can honor and celebrate the work that has been done. And this is what gives me the hope and the conviction to keep doing my part to bring about a day when no American should have to take a knee to bring attention to grave, ongoing injustice. A lot of progress has been made— that's the beauty of where we are today. But a lot is still ahead of us. At least in Atlanta, we have the advantage of having the shoulders of civil rights giants to stand on.

||||||||||||||||||||

You Only Pass Through Once

A life is not important except in the impact it has on other lives.

—JACKIE ROBINSON

"Please ask Angie to join us on the phone."

As soon as my old friend Dr. Bruce Green uttered those words, I knew the news was bad. Once we were both on the line, he delivered the message I'd been dreading: I had prostate cancer. He hastened to add that it was a treatable form of the disease, and my prognosis was good. But there's no real way to soften the blow of the c-word. Cancer is the second-leading cause of death for men in the United States, affecting hundreds of thousands every year. At the age of seventy-three, despite a healthy and active lifestyle, I found myself among their numbers.

My first thought, after the shock of the news subsided a little, was of my family. How was I going to tell them? The next few months were a whirlwind of information, doctors' appointments, and tough choices. Angie never left my side throughout, and eventually we made the decision to pursue an aggressive treatment that included surgery. I was blessed to be treated by one of the best doctors in the world, Dr. Ash Tewari at New York's Mount Sinai Hospital.

Most people who've received a cancer diagnosis will tell you that it is an immediate wake-up call. Life is short—we hear it all the time, but do we believe it? For me, the diagnosis was a further encouragement to reassess my priorities at that stage of my life. I'd recently made the decision to take a step back from the day-to-day running of our for-profit businesses, passing the CEO role for our Atlanta-based companies into the capable hands of Steve Cannon. Cancer or no cancer, I intended to devote more time to my family and to the things that brought me internal happiness and peace. I'd even been learning to meditate, with expert coaching from my friend Deepak Chopra. I also wanted to give more attention to the foundation and accelerate our giving. Now, my health became paramount as well. However, I had no intention of abandoning my active role with the businesses. Besides my family, those are the things that I live for, that bring me a sense of purpose and fulfillment.

As I've shared in these pages, I often ask our associates: Is this organization worthy of your life? Does the place where you're spending so many of your days and the values it stands for provide you with a sense of meaning and purpose? After my cancer diagnosis, I found myself reflecting on that question in relationship to my own life. I've lived a full life, but I cannot pretend it has been entirely a balanced one. I've worked hard and been driven for decades. But when I look back, I find few regrets. I've been blessed with a wonderful family and a rich tapestry of relationships, both personal and professional, that have uplifted and inspired me. And I have no doubt that the organizations I've built have been—and continue to be—worthy of the effort and investment I've put in.

Each of them is so different, and yet the values that form the bedrock for each are the same. Each of them continues, in its own unique way, to provide value to its founders; its associates; its customers, guests, or fans; its community; and its industry. Each tells a story about the potential of business that stands in contrast to the prevailing narrative. And taken together, I hope these stories may do their part to chip away at the pervasive myth that profit is at odds with purpose. Businesses *can* be a powerful force for good in the world. They can and they should serve people, not the other way around. When good companies put the well-being of their customers, their associates, and their communities first, financial success will follow. Values-driven capitalism is good for the bottom line and for society.

There's Enough Pie for Everyone

Black, brown, chestnut, buckskin, gray, roan, palomino, paint—the horses' coats form a moving patchwork, tinted pink by the setting sun, as they mill anxiously in the corral. Kids in cowboy boots and hats scramble to higher ground, where they can get a better view. Parents ready their cameras. Young men and women on horseback circle by the gate. And then it's open. The sound of hoofbeats fills the tranquil valley as the wranglers gallop ahead and the herd surges into the green pasture. Guests gasp in delight as the dozens of horses that have carried them on the two-hour ride down from the ranch run free in the evening light, their work done for the day. For many, this finale of our traditional Dinner Ride is the highlight of their stay at Mountain Sky.

I've been fortunate enough to visit many beautiful parts of the world, but it's hard to think of anywhere that surpasses Montana's Paradise Valley. As many times as I've witnessed it, I never tire of the stunning scenery and the spectacle of the horses enjoying their well-earned time off. But my personal favorite moment comes just before we release the horses. When the grills are finally turned off and the plates are empty, I head over to the picnic area and take my place behind a table laden with pies. Often, a couple of my kids join me, and all our guests line up for dessert. I'll offer each of them a choice of pie—blueberry, cherry, coconut cream, key lime, chocolate cream, peach, strawberry-rhubarb, apple, pumpkin, pecan. If they can't choose, they can come back for more! Returning guests know the drill and look forward to it—as do I. New guests are often surprised to find the owner and his family serving them. But there are few things in life that give me more satisfaction than this simple act of service.

When I was just a kid, my mother would sometimes take Michael and me to Times Square and let us choose a slice of pie at the Automat. That ultra-modern dining experience had no visible servers—just a wall of little boxes with glass windows displaying the food. It was like magic—you picked your flavor, put a nickel in the slot, and opened a little door to remove your prize. These days, I appreciate the magic in the human element—that moment of connection that is forged between two people as one hands the other a delicious slice of pie. This is the essence of doing good business—not transactions but relationships. The currency being exchanged is not just money but happiness. Every time I serve the pie, I feel connected to the same spirit with which our orange-aproned associates light up the aisles at The Home Depot; the same energy with which our game-day staff welcome tens of thousands to the stadium; the same care with which our sales associates at PGA TOUR Superstore treat every customer, young and old. And when our guests smile and take their piece of pie to share with their families and loved ones, I see the same joy we seek to inspire in our fans, our customers, our grantees, our nonprofit guests at West Creek, and everyone else our businesses touch. It doesn't take much to spark that positive response in another human being. But it means everything.

Ultimately, this intangible but invaluable increase in human happiness is the legacy I hope to leave. It's not the buildings or the businesses or the bank accounts, although all of that is wonderful and essential to the continuation of this work. My hoped-for legacy is our values, and the people those values live on in—my children, our associates, and, hopefully, people I've never met who will read this book and be inspired to build values-driven businesses.

When I think about the divisiveness that is too prevalent today in our country and our world, it saddens me. What makes this country great is its diversity, and the opportunities it provides for people of many different races and backgrounds to work together and create something greater than any one of us could do alone. I won't deny that there are deep inequities in our society, and much work needs to be done in order to make opportunity available to all. But I don't subscribe to the notion that there is not enough to go around or that one person's or group's success must come at the expense of another. Too many are quick to blame corporations, or the system of capitalism as a whole, for the ills that beset our society. But capitalism—when grounded in positive values like service, care, and giving back—is what lifts people out of poverty and creates more opportunity for more people. Every good company creates a ripple effect of enrichment and upliftment. When I think about my grandparents coming to this country with nothing but the clothes on their backs and building a life for their children through their own hard work and commitment, I'm inspired. When I think of my father creating a business that allowed him to work for himself and support his family, and my mother taking over that business and building it into a valuable asset that allowed her to give my brother and me a great education and to extend her generous spirit to more people, I'm humbled and grateful. When I think about The Home Depot—that concept that Bernie and I first sketched out on yellow legal pads at a coffee shop—I can hardly believe how far those ripples have reached.

Back in the early eighties, shortly after we went public, Bernie and I were driving to visit one of our stores. I looked across at him and suddenly it hit me how crazy it all was. I elbowed him sharply. "Can you believe this? How did we do this? How did we get here?" We both started laughing in sheer amazement at our good fortune. Little did we know that we were just getting started.

The Home Depot created jobs and pathways to opportunity for hundreds of thousands of people, many of whom have gone on to establish their own foundations and continue the spirit of giving. It has contributed hundreds of millions of dollars to worthy causes. It has blessed its founders beyond our wildest dreams, and I'm proud to say that my partners have used that good fortune in a wonderful variety of ways to continue spreading wealth and opportunity. Bernie Marcus has done extraordinary work in founding the Marcus Autism Center, funding state-of-the-art medical research and facilities, and providing critical support for veterans with traumatic brain injuries. He has joined me in signing the Giving Pledge, committing the majority of his wealth to philanthropic causes. He and I have come full circle and are so happy to be working together again, this time on joint philanthropic ventures. Ken Langone recently made a $100 million donation to help NYU School of Medicine go completely tuition-free, saving the country's future doctors and nurses from beginning their careers mired in debt, and opening the doors of the school to previously underrepresented groups. Since leaving The Home Depot, I've created businesses that employ thousands of people and touch the lives of hundreds of thousands more. Our teams bring excitement and connection to their fans and have energized our great city. Our stores bring joy and healthy activity into people's lives. Our ranches connect families to the beauty of the natural environment and to one another. Every business gives its associates opportunities to give and to make a difference. And the success of all those businesses feeds our family foundation, which has given away nearly $600 million to date and is growing every year. The ripples continue to spread.

I'm encouraged when I speak to young people today, whether they're my own children, our associates, or the business school students I'm sometimes invited to address. I see a bigger vision in them than I did in my own generation, and a more awakened sense of responsibility for social justice, democracy, human rights, and the well-being of our planet. They see what's wrong with our world today; I just hope they don't allow the reality of those problems to dampen their sense of optimism and possibility. Yes, we have a long way to go, and we'll always have issues to address. The work of repairing the world is never done—there truly is no finish line in that journey. But we each can make a difference, and it's a great joy and a privilege to be able to do that, for the time we each have on this earth.

My cancer surgery in 2016 was successful, and today I am grateful to be free of the disease. But I realize that I will never completely go back to the person I once was, physically, emotionally, or spiritually. Like many survivors, I came out of the ordeal with a deeper appreciation for the preciousness of life and a renewed commitment to make every moment count. In her memoir, my mother, Molly, quoted a wise old saying: "I expect to pass through this world but once. Any good, therefore, that I can do, or any kindness that I can show to any fellow creature, let me do it now. Let me not defer nor neglect it, for I shall not pass this way again." True to those words, Molly lived until she was just shy of one hundred with her own inimitable blend of passion and toughness. I have also done my best to live my life by this creed, and since my own mortality has become more vivid to me, so too have those words: *We only pass through once.*

For me, however, that sentiment is always held in contrast with my other favorite saying: *There is no finish line.* While my time in this human body will be finite, my sense of purpose extends far beyond the limits of my own lifetime. In the journey we're all on, as a species and as a planet, there truly is no end in sight. We've taken tremendous strides forward, and we have so much further to go. But I'm optimistic we'll make progress, together.

I deeply believe that we live in an abundant world—one in which there is enough for everyone. Humanity is rich in ingenuity, talent, and resources. As a species, we have proven our resilience time and time again, and we continue to make measurable improvements on a global and national scale in lifting people out of poverty, providing education, and opening doors of opportunity. The key that unlocks this abundance is our values—the principles that guide us in business and in life. If our enterprises are rooted in values like those I've outlined in this book, they will be a force for good and will become role models for others to follow. There is enough pie for everyone. And good companies—values-driven companies—continue to make the pie bigger.

Photo Credits

All interior images courtesy of AMBSE Creative.

All photos in the insert are courtesy of the author except for those listed below:

Page 1: Jimmy Cribb/AMBSE Creative

Page 2, top: David Turpen

Page 2, bottom: Kara Durrette/AMBSE Creative

Page 3: Courtesy of The Home Depot Archives

Page 4, top and middle: Morgan Lee Pearson

Page 4, bottom: Carmen Mandato/AMBSE Creative

Page 5, top: Karl Moore/AMBSE Creative

Page 5, middle: AJ Reynolds/AMBSE Creative

Page 5, bottom: David Kosmos Smith/AMBSE Creative

Page 6, top and bottom: Michael Benford/AMBSE Creative

Page 6, middle: Jacob Gonzalez/AMBSE Creative

Page 7, top: David Turpen

Page 8, top: Art of Life Photography/PGA TOUR Superstore

Page 8, middle: Allie Jest/NFL

Page 8, bottom: Dustin Chambers

Notes

Introduction

1. Ghassan Khoury and Steve Crabtree, "Are Businesses Worldwide Suffering from a Trust Crisis?," Gallup, February 6, 2019, https://www.gallup.com/workplace/246194/businesses-worldwide-suffering-trust-crisis.aspx.

2. Lee Rainie, Scott Keeter, and Andrew Perrin, "Trust and Distrust in America," Pew Research Center, July 22, 2019, https://www.people-press.org/2019/07/22/trust-and-distrust-in-america.

Chapter 1: Family Business

1. *2019 Edelman Trust Barometer Executive Summary*, Edelman Trust Barometer, 2019, https://www.edelman.com/sites/g/files/aatuss191/files/2019-01/2019_Edelman_Trust_Barometer_Executive_Summary.pdf.

2. "Business Roundtable Redefines the Purpose of a Corporation to Promote 'An Economy That Serves All Americans,'" Business Roundtable, August 19, 2019, https://www.businessroundtable.org/business-round table-redefines-the-purpose-of-a-corporation-to-promote-an-economy-that-serves-all-americans.

Chapter 3: You're Only as Good as Your People

1. Simon Sinek, *Leaders Eat Last* (New York: Portfolio, 2017), 222.

2. "State of the American Workplace," Gallup, 2017, https://www.gallup.com/workplace/238085/state-american-workplace-report-2017.aspx.

3. Robert Armstrong, Eric Platt, and Oliver Ralph, "Warren Buffett: 'I'm Having More Fun Than Any 88-Year-Old in the World,'" *Financial Times,* April 24, 2019, https://www.ft.com/content/40b9b356-661e-11e9-a79d-04f350474d62.

4. Harvard Study of Adult Development, https://www.adultdevelopment study.org.

5. Robert Waldinger, "What Makes a Good Life? Lessons from the Longest Study on Happiness," TEDxBeaconStreet, November 2015, https://www.ted.com/talks/robert_waldinger_what_makes_a_good_life_les sons_from_the_longest_study_on_happiness.

6. Annie Dillard, *The Writing Life* (New York: Harper Perennial, 2013), 32.

7. Sarabjit Singh Baveja, Sharad Rastogi, Chris Zook, Randall S. Hancock, and Julian Chu, "The Value of Online Customer Loyalty and How You Can Capture It: eStrategy Brief," Bain & Company and Mainspring,

http://www2.bain.com/Images/Value_online_customer_loyalty_you
_capture.pdf.

Chapter 6: Good Companies Make Good Neighbors

1. Jill Lepore, "Reigns of Terror in America," *New Yorker*, November 4, 2018, https://www.newyorker.com/magazine/2018/11/12/reigns-of-terror
-in-america.

2. Martin Luther King Jr., "Address Delivered at the National Biennial Convention of the American Jewish Congress," Miami Beach, FL, May 14, 1958, https://kinginstitute.stanford.edu/king-papers/docu ments/address-delivered-national-biennial-convention-american-jew ish-congress.

3. Sarah Foster and Wei Lu, "Atlanta Ranks Worst in Income Inequality in the U.S.," *Bloomberg*, October 10, 2018, https://www.bloomberg .com/news/articles/2018-10-10/atlanta-takes-top-income-inequality
-spot-among-american-cities.

4. Charles Davidson, "Economist Examines Inequality of Opportunity," *Economy Matters*, Federal Reserve Bank of Atlanta, November 1, 2018, https://www.frbatlanta.org/economy-matters/community-and-economic
-development/2018/11/01/economist-examines-inequality-of-opportu nity.

5. Abraham Joshua Heschel, "The Reasons for My Involvement in the Peace Movement," *Journal of Social Philosophy* 4, no. 1 (January 1973): 7–8; later included in *Moral Grandeur and Spiritual Audacity* (New York: Farrar, Straus and Giroux, 1996).

6. Abraham Joshua Heschel, "Religion and Race," Voices of Democracy: The U.S. Oratory Project, January 14, 1963, https://voicesofdemocracy .umd.edu/heschel-religion-and-race-speech-text.

7. Elly Yu, "An Atlanta Neighborhood Tries to Redefine Gentrification," *Code Switch*, NPR, September 23, 2015, https://www.npr.org /sections/codeswitch/2015/09/23/435293852/an-atlanta-neighbor hood-tries-to-redefine-gentrification.

8. East Lake Foundation, "Our Impact: Overview," https://www.eastlake foundation.org/our-impact/overview.

9. Ken Belson, "Building a Stadium, Rebuilding a Neighborhood," *New York Times*, January 12, 2017, https://www.nytimes.com/2017/01/12 /sports/football/atlanta-falcons-stadium-arthur-blank-neighborhood .html.

10. Randall Lane, "Bill Gates: My New Model for Giving," *Forbes*, September 18, 2012, https://www.forbes.com/sites/randalllane/2012/09/18/bill
-gates-my-new-model-for-giving/#44a07fe275ec.

11. Dennis R. Young, "An Interview with Ambassador Andrew Young,"

Nonprofit Policy Forum 1, no. 1, article 7 (2010): 1–12, DOI: 10.2202/2154-3348.1009.

12. Ibid.

Chapter 7: You Always Get More Than You Give

1. Brian O'Connell, "The Search for Meaning," Society for Human Resource Management, March 23, 2019, https://www.shrm.org/hr-today/news/all-things-work/pages/the-search-for-meaning.aspx.

2. Tammy Erickson, "Meaning Is the New Money," *Harvard Business Review,* March 23, 2011, https://hbr.org/2011/03/challenging-our-deeply-held-as.

3. Elizabeth Schwinn, "Big-Sky Philanthropy," *Chronicle of Philanthropy,* April 6, 2006, https://www.philanthropy.com/article/Big-Sky-Philanthropy/172499.

Chapter 8: We Want the Wheels to Wobble (a Little)

1. Ryan Wallerson, "Youth Participation Weakens in Basketball, Football, Baseball, Soccer: Fewer Children Play Team Sports," *Wall Street Journal,* January 31, 2014, http://online.wsj.com/news/articles/SB10001424052702303519404579350892629229918.

2. Doug McIntyre, "All-Access Atlanta: How United Are on Track to Be the Most Successful Expansion Team in MLS History," ESPN, http://www.espn.com/espn/feature/story/_/id/19211839/all-access-atlanta-how-united-track-most-successful-expansion-team-mls-history.

Chapter 10: From Protest to Progress

1. Arnie Stapleton, "Don't Talk about Mom: NFL Players Angry over Trump's Insult," AP News, September 25, 2017, https://apnews.com/e26b0c8327ee4e00931f6fe96def97a0/Don't-talk-about-mom:-NFL-players-angry-over-Trump's-insult.

Index